Fodor's

CW01068545

Vienna

Reprinted from *Fodor's Austria '90*

FODOR'S TRAVEL PUBLICATIONS, INC.
New York & London

ISBN 0–679–01844–1

Fodor's Vienna

Editor: Richard Moore
Area Editor: George W. Hamilton
Editorial Contributors: Nicholas Allen, Mark Lewes, Kenneth Loveland

Drawings: Keith Howard
Maps Swanston Graphics, Bryan Woodfield
Cover Photograph: S. Franklin/Magnum

Cover Design: Vignelli Associates

Special Sales

Fodor's Travel Publications are available at special discounts for bulk purchases
(100 copies or more) for sales promotions or premiums. Special editions,
including personalized covers, excerpts of existing guides, and corporate
imprints, can be created in large quantities for special needs. For more
information, write to Special Marketing, Fodor's Travel Publications, Inc., 201
East 50th Street, New York 10022. Enquiries from the United Kingdom should
be sent to Fodor's Travel Publications, 30–32 Bedford Square, London WC1B
3SG.

MANUFACTURED IN THE UNITED STATES OF AMERICA
10 9 8 7 6 5 4 3 2 1

CONTENTS

FOREWORD

Vienna is a city in which it is impossible to avoid almost hourly contact with the very fabric of history. Once the heart of a vast empire that stretched to the New World, Vienna today is an attractive amalgam of the rich vestiges of its proud past and a dynamic and progressive approach to the modern world. It is home to both the Hofburg, with its Burgundian treasures, and the U.N.O. city, which houses the International Atomic Energy Agency as well as the U.N. Industrial Development Organization and other U.N. offices.

The city is poised at the very heart of the Continent, sharing its cultural heritage with both northern and southern Europe, and yet having obvious affinities with lands beyond. It was Metternich who said that "Asia begins at the Landstrasse," encapsulating thus the critical role of Vienna as the meeting place of East and West for 2,000 years.

It goes without saying that the city has an old-world charm—a fact which the Viennese are both ready to acknowledge and yet hate being told. It is possible to wander its elegant streets, take coffee in its historic coffee-houses, or spend an evocative evening in a wine cellar, deep under ground, and imagine yourself in a time when tourism was still "travel" and visitors to a foreign land were greeted with courtesy and dignified charm. Even in winter, when the bitter winds blow damp fogs through the canyoned streets, and you find yourself looking with sympathy at a shivering cab horse, the city can still reveal a warmth and friendliness all too rare today. In summer, when the street cafés spill out over the pedestrian malls, and you can take to the Vienna Woods to drink cool white wine under the stars, the ancient capital of the Habsburgs can still work its spell.

Vienna has a great deal to see and do, and—especially to anyone who can receive signals from distant times—seeing and doing takes on a new dimension here.

*

We would like to thank the Director of the Austrian National Tourist Office in Vienna and his staff for their considerable help and interest; Director Werner Fritz of the London office and his staff for their unfailing courtesy; and George W. Hamilton for his unflagging help and expertise.

*

We would like to stress that the hotel and restaurant listings in this guide are *not exhaustive:* we do not profess to provide a complete listing for accommodations or for eating places. We select those we feel would interest our readers, and change that listing year by year.

While every care has been taken to assure the accuracy of the information in this guide, the passage of time will always bring change, and consequently the publisher cannot accept responsibility for errors that may occur.

All prices and opening times quoted in this guide are based on information available to us at press time. Hours and admission fees may change, however, and the prudent traveler will avoid inconvenience by calling ahead.

Fodor's wants to hear about your travel experiences, both pleasant and unpleasant. When a hotel or restaurant fails to live up to its billing, let us know and we will investigate the complaint and revise our entries where the facts warrant it.

Send your letters to the editors or Fodor's Travel Publications, 201 E. 50th Street, New York, NY 10022.

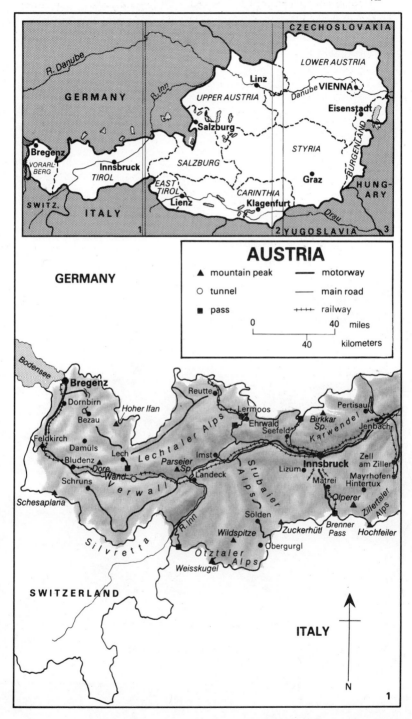

AUSTRIA

- ▲ mountain peak
- ○ tunnel
- ■ pass

- ━━ motorway
- ── main road
- ++++ railway

0   40 miles

40 kilometers

GERMANY

CZECHOSLOVAKIA

R. Danube

GERMANY

R. Inn

LOWER AUSTRIA

Linz

Danube VIENNA

UPPER AUSTRIA

Eisenstadt

Salzburg

STYRIA

BURGENLAND

Bregenz

VORARL-
BERG

Innsbruck

TIROL

SALZBURG

SWITZ.

ITALY

EAST
TIROL

Lienz

CARINTHIA

Klagenfurt

Graz

HUNG-
ARY

Drau

YUGOSLAVIA

Bodensee

Bregenz

Dornbirn

Bezau

Hoher Ifan

Reutte

Lermoos

Ehrwald

Seefeld

Pertisau

Birkkar
Sp.

Karwendel

Jenbach

Feldkirch

Damüls

Lech

Lechtaler Alps

Imst

Lizum

Innsbruck

Zell
am Ziller

Bludenz

Dore
Wand

Parseier
Sp.

Landeck

Stubaier

Matrei

Mayrhofen

Hintertux

Schruns

Verwall

Olperer

Zillertaler
Alps

Schesaplana

R. Inn

Sölden

Alps

Brenner
Pass

Hochfeiler

Silvretta

Wildspitze

Zuckerhütl

Obergurgl

Ötztaler
Alps

SWITZERLAND

Weisskugel

ITALY

N

1

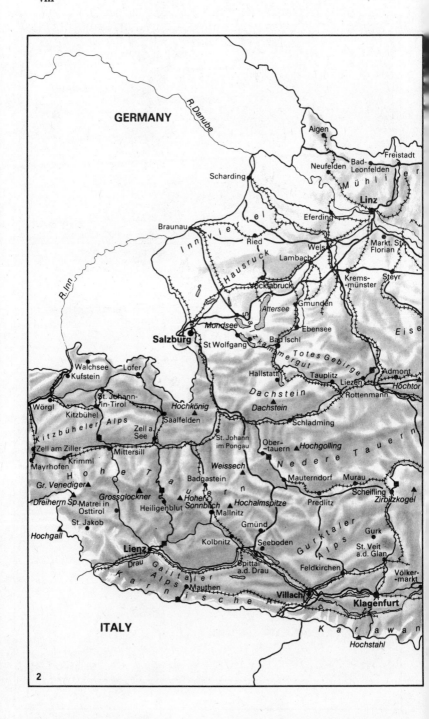

GERMANY

R.Danube

Aigen

Neufelden
Bad-
Leonfelden
Freistadt

Scharding

Mühli...

Linz

Eferding

Braunau

Inn viertel

Ried

Wels

Markt. St.
Florian

Hausruck

Lambach

Krems-
münster

Steyr

Vöcklabruck

R.Inn

Attersee

Gmunden

Eise...

Mondsee

Salzburg

St Wolfgang

Bad Ischl

Ebensee

St kammergut

Totes Gebirge

Admont

Hallstatt

Tauplitz

Liezen

Höchtor

Walchsee

Lofer

Dachstein

Rottenmann

Kufstein

Dachstein

Schladming

Wörgl

St. Johann-
in-Tirol

Hochkönig

Kitzbühel

Kitzbüheler Alps

Saalfelden

Zell a.
See

St. Johann
im Pongau

Ober-
tauern

Hochgolling

Nedere Tauern

Zell am Ziller

Mittersill

Hohe Tauern

Weissech

Mauterndorf

Murau

Krimml

Scheifling

Mayrhofen

Badgastein

Zirbitzkogel

Gr. Venediger

Grossglockner

Hoher
Sonnblich

Hochalmspitze

Predlitz

Dreiherrn Sp.

Matrei in
Osttirol

Heiligenblut

Mallnitz

Gmünd

Gurktaler

Gurk

St. Jakob

Gurk

St. Veit
a.d. Glan

Hochgall

Kolbnitz

Seeboden

Alps

Lienz

Drau

Gailtaler Alps

Spittal
a.d. Drau

Feldkirchen

Völker-
markt

Karnische A...

Mauthen

Villach

Klagenfurt

ITALY

Karawan...

Hochstahl

2

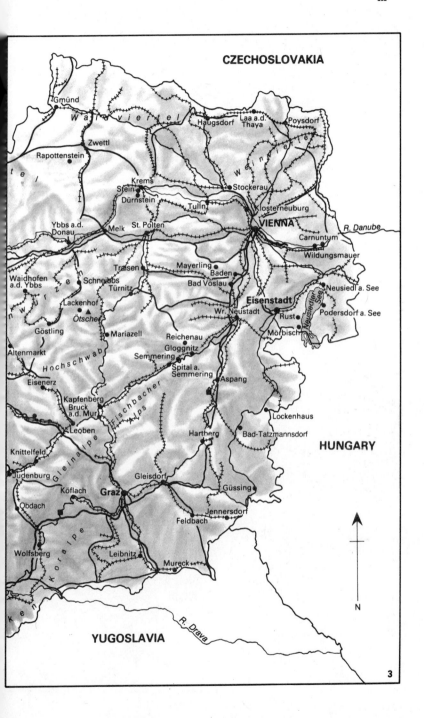

CZECHOSLOVAKIA

Gmünd

Waldviertel

Zwettl

Rapottenstein

Haugsdorf   Laa a.d.   Poysdorf
Thaya

Weinviertel

Krems   Stockerau
Stein
Dürnstein   Tulln
Klosterneuburg

Ybbs a.d.   Melk   St. Pölten   VIENNA
Donau   R. Danube

Carnuntum

Wildungsmauer

Traisen   Mayerling   Baden
Waidhofen   Schneibbs   Bad Vöslau
a.d. Ybbs   Türnitz
Lackenhof   Eisenstadt   Neusiedl a. See
Ötscher   Wr. Neustadt   Rust   Podersdorf a. See
Göstling   Mariazell   Mörbisch
Altenmarkt   Reichenau
Hochschwab   Gloggnitz
Semmering
Eisenerz   Spital a.
Semmering   Aspang
Kapfenberg
Bruck   Fischbacher Alps   Lockenhaus
a.d. Mur
Leoben   Hartberg   Bad-Tatzmannsdorf
Knittelfeld   HUNGARY
Judenburg   Gleinalpe
Köflach   Graz   Gleisdorf   Güssing
Obdach   Jennersdorf
Feldbach
Koralpe
Wolfsberg   Leibnitz   Mureck

N

R. Drava

YUGOSLAVIA

3

FACTS AT YOUR FINGERTIPS

FACTS AT YOUR FINGERTIPS

Planning Your Trip

SOURCES OF INFORMATION. In the U.S. The major source of information for anyone planning a vacation to Austria is the *Austrian National Tourist Office,* 500 Fifth Ave., 20th Floor, New York, NY 10110 (212–944–6880); 11601 Wilshire Blvd., Suite 2480, Los Angeles, CA 90025 (213–477–3332); 4800 San Felipe, Suite 500, Houston, TX 77056 (713–850–9999); 500 N. Michigan Ave., Suite 544, Chicago, IL 60611 (312–644–5556). They can supply information on all aspects of travel to and around the country, from which type of vacation is best suited to your needs and purse, to the best and most economical ways of getting around. They will also have a wealth of material on hotels, restaurants, excursions, museums and so on. They produce copious amounts of information, much of it free and all of it useful.

In Canada contact the Tourist Bureaus at 736 Granville St., Suite 1220, Vancouver Block, Vancouver BC V6Z 1J2 (604–683–8695); 2 Bloor St. E., Suite 3330, Toronto, Ontario M4W 1A8 (416–967–3348); 1010 Sherbrooke St. W., Suite 1410, Montreal, Quebec H3A 2R7 (514–849–3709). The office also offers a snow-conditions report during the season—phone 416–967–6870.

In the U.K. the address is—30 St. George St., London W1R OAL (01–629 0461). The office also runs a jazzily-named *Holiday Hotline* for the latest resort and price information—phone 01–629 0461.

WHEN TO GO. Austria has two main seasons. The **summer season** starts at Easter and ends about the middle of October. May, June, September and October are the pleasantest for traveling about (except in Vienna), sufficiently warm, and there is less competition for hotel rooms and restaurant tables; also prices tend to be lower.

June through August are the most crowded months, when the main festivals take place. The Vienna Festival is from mid-May to the end of June; the Schubert Festival in Hohenems, Vorarlberg, is in mid-June; the Carinthian Summer Festival is in July and August; and the Salzburg, Bregenz and Mörbisch Festivals are in late July and August. Less international, the Bruckner Festival in Linz and St. Florian is in September; and the Styrian Autumn Festival is from the beginning of October to mid-November.

The **water-sports season** also, obviously, has its peak in July and August when the beaches of the Carinthian lakes, Bodensee (Lake Constance) in Vorarlberg, and Neusiedlersee in Burgenland are positively swarming with swimmers. The waters of the Salzkammergut lakes are cooler, but they have just as much sailing and boating. Water-ski contests are a regular feature on the principal lakes, and on Wörthersee in Carinthia you can see occasionally night water-ski jumping with torches. The summer season

1

in the principal lake resorts is very lively as it is also in the principal spas, such as Bad Hofgastein, Badgastein, Bad Ischl, and Baden near Vienna. In all these places, however, you have to make your reservations well in advance. Even the smallest resort features an openair swimming pool; most better resort hotels have one, many two, indoor and outdoor pools.

The year kicks off with high jinks at Carnival, or Fasching, when celebrations start and crescendo towards Ash Wednesday. They include hundreds of balls in Vienna, most notably the Philharmonic Ball on Jan. 18, and the grand gala Opera Ball on Feb. 22 this year.

CLIMATE. The traditional four seasons. Generally speaking Austria has a moderate Central European climate. However, as the altitude and general geographical situation vary tremendously from one part of the country to another, it is always wise to check up locally. This is especially true in the winter, when road conditions can be very dangerous due to ice, snow and fog.

Average maximum afternoon temperatures in degrees Fahrenheit and Centigrade:

Vienna	Jan.	Feb.	Mar.	Apr.	May	June	July	Aug.	Sept.	Oct.	Nov.	Dec.
F°	34	38	47	57	66	71	75	73	66	55	44	37
C°	1	3	8	14	19	22	24	23	19	13	7	3

WHAT TO PACK. There is really only one supreme rule—travel light. This makes more sense than ever now that any journey may suddenly be made more complicated by strikes of baggage handlers at airports. If you realize that what ever you take you may have to carry yourself, then you will be surprised to find how much you can leave at home!

For transatlantic travelers by air the regulations should be noted carefully. Your baggage is subject to a size allowance, not a weight one. First-class passengers may have two pieces of baggage, provided that the total of the height, width and length does not exceed 124 inches (316 cm.). Economy-class passengers may also have two pieces of baggage, but the total sum of their height, length and width must not exceed 106 inches (270 cm.) and neither of the two must exceed a total of 62 inches (155 cm.). All other passengers (i.e. non-transatlantic ones), are still bound by the weight limitations of 66 lb. in First Class and 44 lb. in Economy.

It's a good idea to pack the bulk of your things in one bag and put everything you need for overnight, or for two or three nights, in a carry-on bag, to obviate packing and repacking at brief stops. Motorists will find it advisable to be frugal as well. You should limit your luggage to what can be locked into the trunk or boot of your car when making daytime stops.

Take what you would wear for the same sort of activities you plan to indulge in if you were staying in Britain or the northern United States. Remember, however, that if you are going to investigate any high altitudes (and it's pretty hard in Austria not to), you will find evenings chilly even in midsummer, so a warm sweater or two is a good thing to have. If you are going in for sports, the same sort of sports clothes you wear at home will be appropriate. Do take comfortable walking shoes; women's shoes need to have broad heels to cope with the diminutive cobblestones of many Austrian city streets.

If you plan to spend much time in cities or the better resorts and go to top-notch places, you will find Austrians more formal, on the whole, than Americans and Britons, and you had better take some evening clothes, or at least fairly sober ones. Even in the summer, gala performances at the festivals tend to be dressy affairs.

COSTS IN AUSTRIA. Austria remains one of Europe's best buys. While not inexpensive, Vienna still offers value for money. Generally, prices directly concerned with tourism (hotels, ski-lifts and restaurants) have, despite high taxes, have increased less than in other major tourist countries.

Vienna and Salzburg lead the list of expensive cities in Austria, followed by Innsbruck. Expensive resorts include Kitzbühel, Seefeld, Badgastein, Bad Hofgastein, Velden, Saalbach, Zell am See, Pörtschach.

Farther down the ledger, there are many old and attractive towns and cities (Graz, Linz, Krems, Hallstatt, Feldkirch, Dürnstein, Steyr to mention a few) which offer almost as much history and notable architecture in attractive and comfortable surroundings, but at much lower cost.

Hotels. Austrian hotels are officially classified from one to five stars according to strict government standards and inspection. In order to give our readers a clearer picture, in regard to prices as well as quality, we have employed our own classification, dividing hotels into four categories. They are: for a double room—*Luxury* AS2,000–4,000; *Expensive* AS1,500–2,200; *Moderate* AS900–1,500; and *Inexpensive* AS500–900. For a single—*Luxury* AS1,500–2,500; *Expensive* AS1,000–1,500; *Moderate* AS600–1,000; and *Inexpensive* AS300–600.

Restaurants. We grade the restaurants in our listing as—*Expensive* AS500 and up, way up, and this is without wine; *Moderate* AS300–500; and *Inexpensive* AS150–300. The *Inexpensive* is a wildly variable category, and if you have the set menu at lunchtime (the Austrians' main meal) you could easily eat inexpensively in a distinctly moderate spot. The prices are for one person, without wine.

Off-season travel is recommended if you are willing to pass up the big events, which necessarily take place in the main season, and are free to take your trip at any time of the year. It is cheaper—air fares and hotel rates are lower out of season. Lower hotel charges off season are very frequent in Austria, especially on full board terms, sometimes amounting to as much as 33 1/3% and even more. Even where prices are the same, you get better accommodations: the choicest rooms in the hotels and the best tables in the restaurants have not been pre-empted and train compartments are not jammed full.

Warning: Other Nasty Taxes. The tax situation becomes more complicated when it comes to beverages: there is, *in addition* to the Value Added Tax, a beverage or refreshment tax, which also applies to ice cream and coffee; then there is an alcohol tax added to beer, wine and liquor; and, finally, champagne gets hit with still another champagne tax. Thus drinking anything but water in Austria (which fortunately is very good) can be an expensive pastime. All these taxes are *included* automatically in the price, so you will not notice them as a separate imposition, but they are there all the same.

Sample costs. It will cost about AS50 to have a shirt laundered; from AS120 to dryclean a suit, and from AS70 a dress; a shampoo and set for a woman will cost her around AS400, a manicure from AS60; a man's haircut (without shampoo) from AS100.

Opera tickets cost from AS80–2,000 (Salzburg Festival up to AS3,000), more for special performances; theater tickets from AS50–600.

Some other, liquid, costs are—a bottle of wine costs about AS180–300 (more, of course, for special vintages), but the open wines are very good and cost about AS25–45 per 1/4 liter carafe; a glass (half liter) of beer varies from AS20 to AS30 depending on the establishment; coffee ranges from AS20 to AS40; whiskey about AS55–90; schnapps AS15–30; a cocktail in a top bar will cost at least AS90; mineral water, apple juice, Coca-Cola, and similar drinks run at about AS19; all these are inclusive of taxes.

TAKING MONEY ABROAD. Traveler's checks are still the standard and best way to safeguard your travel funds; and you will usually get as good a rate of exchange in Austria for traveler's checks as you will for cash. In the U.S., many of the larger banks issue their own traveler's checks—just about as universally recognized as those of American Express, Cook and Barclays—as well as those of one or more of the other firms mentioned. In most instances there is a 1% charge for the checks; there is no fee for Barclays checks. Some banks also issue them free if you are a regular customer. The best-known British checks are Cook's and those of Barclays, Lloyds, Midland and National Westminster banks. It is also always a good idea to have some local currency upon arrival for the airport bus, taxis, tips and so on. Some banks will provide this service; alternatively, contact Deak International Ltd., 630 Fifth Ave., New York, NY 10111 (212–635–0515, call for additional locations). But try to get bills in smaller denominations—it is embarrassing to have local currency which you can't use.

Britons holding a Uniform Eurocheque card and check book—apply for them at your bank—can cash checks for up to £100 a day at banks participating in the scheme *and* write checks for goods and services (hotels, restaurants, shops, etc.) again up to £100.

CREDIT CARDS. Credit cards are now an integral part of the Western Financial Way of Life and, in theory at least, they are accepted all over Europe. In theory, because Austria is one of the countries where they are less used than elsewhere. There are many thrifty Austrian restaurateurs and hoteliers who are damned if they see why they should turn over any part of their hard-earned money to credit card companies, and stoutly refuse to accept plastic payment. A great many of these are the more atmospheric, regional establishments, most likely the very ones you will want to eat in and, in the countryside, stay in. So keep an eye open for those little signs in the window; you could easily find yourself in an embarrassing situation otherwise.

We have included credit card information wherever possible. There are, however, some surprising omissions of hotels or restaurants that you would think would accept credit cards, but don't. The initials we use for this information are AE. DC. MC and V—which stand for American Express, Diner's Club, MasterCard (alias Access and Eurocard) and Visa (Barclaycard in Britain). Be sure to double check that your particular piece of plastic is accepted before ordering a meal or checking into your hotel.

PASSPORTS. All travelers require a passport for entry into Austria. **In the U.S.,** apply in person at U.S. Passport Agency Offices, local county courthouses or selected post offices. If you have a passport not more than eight years old you may apply by mail; otherwise you will need:
1—proof of citizenship, such as a birth certificate;
2—two identical photographs, two inches square, in either black and white or color, on non-glossy paper and taken within the past six months;
3—$35 for the passport itself plus a $7 processing fee if you are applying in person (no processing fee when renewing your passport by mail); for those 18 years and older, or if you are under 18, $20 for the passport plus a $7 processing fee if you are applying in person (again, no extra fee when applying by mail);
4—proof of identity that includes a photo and signature (a driver's license, previous passport or any governmental ID card for example).

Adult passports are valid for 10 years, five years for those 18 and under; they are not renewable. Allow four to six weeks for your application to be processed, but in an emergency, passport agency offices can have a passport readied within 24–48 hours, and even the postal authorities can indicate "Rush" when necessary.

If you expect to travel extensively, request a 48- or 96-page passport rather than the usual 24-page one. There is no extra charge. When you receive your passport, write down its number, date and place of issue separately. The loss of a valid passport should be reported immediately to the local police and to the Passport Office, Department of State, Washington DC 20524. If your passport is lost or stolen while abroad, report it immediately to the local authorities and apply for a replacement at the nearest U.S. Embassy or consular office.

Canadian citizens apply in person to regional passport offices, post offices or by mail to Passport Office, Bureau of Passports, External Affairs, Ottawa, Ontario K1A OG3 (819–994–3500). A $25 fee, two photographs, a guarantor, and evidence of citizenship are required. Canadian passports are valid for five years and are non-renewable.

U.K. citizens. Apply for passports on special forms obtainable from your travel agency or from the main post office in your town. The application should be sent to the passport office in your area (as indicated on the guidance form) or taken personally to your nearest main post office. It is advisable to apply for your passport 4–5 weeks before it is required, although in some cases it will be issued sooner. The regional passport offices are located in London, Liverpool, Peterborough, Glasgow, Newport (Gwent), and Belfast. The application must be countersigned by your bank manager, or by a solicitor, barrister, doctor, clergyman or Justice of the Peace who knows you personally. You will need two photos. The fee is £15. A larger, 94-page passport can be obtained for an extra charge.

British Visitor's Passport. This simplified form of passport has advantages for the once-in-a-while tourist to most European countries (Austria included). Valid for one year and not renewable, it costs £7.50. Application may be made at a local post office (in Northern Ireland at the Passport

Office in Belfast); you will need identification plus two passport photographs—no other formalities.

Visas. Citizens of the United States, Great Britain, and Canada do not
need visas to visit Austria. Citizens of other nations should get in touch
with the nearest Austrian consulate or tourist association representative
for the latest developments on this requirement.

Health Certificates. Not required for entry into Austria. Neither the
United States, Canada nor Great Britain require a certificate of vaccina-
tion prior to re-entry. However, the health regulations can change overnight if there is a scare, so we advise you to check up on the latest status
quo, just in case.

INSURANCE. Travel insurance can cover everything from health and
accident costs, to lost baggage and trip cancellation. Sometimes they can
all be obtained with one blanket policy; other times they overlap with existing coverage you might already have for health and/or home; but there
will be times where it is best to buy policies that are tailored to very specific
needs. Many travelers unwittingly end up with duplicate coverage, so before purchasing separate travel insurance of any kind, check your regular
policies carefully.

Generally, it is best to take care of your insurance needs before embark-
ing on your trip. You'll pay more for less coverage—and have less chance
to read the fine print—if you wait until the last minute and make your
purchases from, say, an airport vending machine or insurance company
counter. If you have a regular insurance agent, that is the person to consult
first.

Flight insurance, which is often included in the price of the ticket when
the fare is paid via American Express, Visa or certain other major credit
cards, is also often included in package policies providing accident coverage as well. These policies are available from most tour operators and insurance companies. While it is a good idea to have health and accident
insurance when traveling, be careful not to spend money to duplicate coverage you may already have . . . or to neglect some eventuality which
could end up costing a small fortune.

For example, basic Blue Cross–Blue Shield policies do cover health
costs incurred while traveling. They will not, however, cover the cost of
emergency transportation, which can often add up to several thousand
dollars. Emergency transportation *is* covered, in part at least, by many
major medical policies such as those underwritten by Prudential and Metropolitan Life. Again, we can't urge you too strongly that in order to be
sure you are getting the coverage you need, check any policy carefully before buying. Another important example: Most insurance issued specifically for travel does not cover pre-existing conditions, such as a heart con-
dition.

Travel Assistance International, the American arm of Europ Assistance,
offers a comprehensive program providing medical and personal emergency services and offering immediate, on-the-spot medical, personal and financial help. Trip protection ranges from $40 for an individual for up to
eight days to $600 for an entire family for a year. Full details from travel
agents or insurance brokers, or from Europ Assistance Worldwide Services, Inc., 1133 15th St., N.W., Suite 400, Washington, DC 20005 (800–

821–2828). In the U.K., contact Europ Assistance Ltd., 252 High St., Croydon, Surrey (01–680 1234).

Carefree Travel Insurance, c/o ARM Coverage Inc., 120 Mineola Blvd., Box 310, Mineola, NY 11501, underwritten by the Hartford Accident and Indemnity Co., offers a comprehensive benefits package that includes trip cancellation and interruption as well as medical, legal and economic assistance. Trip cancellation and interruption insurance can be purchased separately. Call 800–645–2424 for additional information.

International SOS Assistance Inc., Box 11568, Philadelphia, PA 19126 (800–523–8930), has fees from $25 a person for one to thirteen days, to $195 for a year.

IAMAT (International Association for Medical Assistance to Travelers), 417 Center St. Lewiston, NY 14092 (716–754–4883) in the U.S.; or 40 Regal Rd., Guelph, Ontario N1K 1B5 (519–836–0102) in Canada.

The Association of British Insurers, Aldermary House, 10–15 Queen St., London E.C.4 (01–248 4477), will give comprehensive advice on all aspects of vacation travel insurance from the U.K.

Baggage Loss. It is possible, though often a complicated affair, to insure your luggage against loss through theft or negligence. Insurance companies are reluctant to sell such coverage alone, however, since it is often a losing proposition for them. Instead, it is most often included as part of a package that would also cover accidents or health. Remuneration is often determined by weight, regardless of the value of the specific contents of the luggage. Should you lose your luggage or some other personal possession, be sure to report it to the local police immediately. Without documentation of such a report, your insurance company might be very stingy. Also, before buying baggage insurance, check your homeowners policy. Some such policies offer "off-premises theft" coverage, including the loss of luggage while traveling.

Cancellation Coverage. The last major area of traveler's insurance is trip cancellation coverage. This is especially important to travelers on APEX or charter flights. Should you get sick abroad, or for some other reason be unable to continue your trip, you may be stuck having to buy a new one-way fare home, plus paying for space on the charter you're not using. You can guard against this with "trip cancellation insurance," usually available from travel agents. Most of these policies will also cover last minute cancellations.

STUDENT AND YOUTH TRAVEL. All student travelers should obtain an *International Student Identity Card,* which is in most instances needed to get student discounts, youth rail passes, and Intra-European Student Charter Flights. Apply to *Council on International Educational Exchange,* 205 East 42 St., New York, NY 10017. Cost is $10. Canadian students should apply to the *Association of Student Councils,* 187 College St., Toronto, Ontario M5T 1P7. U.K. students should apply to the *National Union of Student Marketing,* 461 Holloway Rd., London N.7 (01–272 9445).

The following organizations can also be helpful in finding student flights, educational opportunities and other information. Most deal with international student travel generally, but materials for those listed cover Austria.

American Youth Hostels, Box 37613, Washington, DC 20013. Members are eligible for entree to the worldwide network of youth hostels. The organization publishes an extensive directory to same.

Council on International Educational Exchange (CIEE), 205 East 42 St., New York, NY 10017 (and 20 satellite offices around the United States called *Council Travel Services*) provides information on summer study, work/travel programs and travel programs and services for college and high school students. CIEE's *Work, Study, Travel Abroad: The Whole World Handbook* ($8.95 plus $1 postage) is the best listing of both work and study possibilities.

Institute of International Education, 809 United Nations Plaza, New York, NY 10017, is primarily concerned with study opportunities and administers scholarships and fellowships for international study and training. The New York office has a visitor's information center; satellite offices are located in Chicago, Denver, Houston, San Francisco and Washington, DC.

Also worth contacting is *Educational Travel Center,* 438 N. Frances St., Madison, WI 53703. Specific information on rail and other discounts is listed in the appropriate sections hereafter.

Among the leading specialists in the field of youth travel are the following:

Arista Student Travel Assoc., Inc., 11 E. 44th St., New York, NY 10017 (212–687–5121).

Bailey Travel Service Inc., 123 E. Market St., York, PA 17401 (717–854–5511).

Campus Holidays, 242 Bellevue Ave., Upper Montclair, NJ 07043 (201–744–8724).

Harwood Tours & Travel, Inc., 2428 Guadalupe, Austin, TX 78705 (512–478–9343).

Osborne Travel Service, Inc., 3379 Peachtree Rd., N.E., Atlanta, GA 30326 (404–261–1608).

In Canada: *Canadian Federation of Student-Services,* 187 College St., Toronto, Ontario M5T 1P7, is a non-profit student service cooperative owned and operated by over 50 college and university student unions. Its travel bureau, *Travel Cuts,* can arrange transportation, tours, and work programs abroad. Try also *Tourbec,* 535 Ontario East, Montreal, Quebec H2L 1N8.

In Britain: Student travel arrangements may be made through the following:

Australian Student Travel, 117 Euston Rd, London NW1.

CTS (Centro Turistico Studentesco—Italian), 33 Windmill St., London W1.

London Student Travel (including Union of Student International Travel—Irish), 52 Grosvenor Gardens, London SW1.

Worldwide Student Travel, 39 Store St., London WC1.

TRAVEL FOR THE DISABLED. Tours specially designed for the disabled generally parallel those of the non-disabled traveler, but at a more leisurely pace. For a complete list of tour operators who arrange such travel write to the *Society for the Advancement of Travel for the Handicapped,*

(SATH), 26 Court St., Brooklyn, NY 11242. Travel Information Service of *Moss Rehabilitation Hospital,* 12th St. and Tabor Road, Philadelphia, PA 19141, answers inquiries regarding specific cities and countries as well as providing toll-free telephone numbers for airlines with special lines for the hearing impaired and, again, listings of selected tour operators.

International Air Transport Association (IATA) publishes a free pamphlet entitled *Incapacitated Passengers' Air Travel Guide.* Write IATA, 2000 Peel Street, Montreal, Quebec H3A 2R4.

From the U.K.: The *Airline Transport Users Committee,* 129 Kingsway, London W.C.2, publish a very useful booklet, *Care In the Air,* free.

But one of the very best guides is a book published by the *Royal Association for Disability and Rehabilitation,* 25 Mortimer St., London W.1, called *Holidays for Disabled People,* £3 from W.H. Smith or direct from RADAR (no charge for post or packing).

Once in Austria, contact *Öst. Zivilinvalidenverband,* Lange Gasse 60, A-1080 Vienna (0222–48 55 05), for further information. A disabled guide to Vienna is available from the *Sozialamt der Stadt Wien,* A-1010, Rathaus.

Staying in Vienna

CUSTOMS ON ARRIVAL. The following is the official list of duty-free items you may bring in with you, but there is no necessity to worry about them unduly. Overworked Austrian customs officials are not especially interested in counting to see that you may have 402 cigarettes with you instead of 400.

Travelers over 17 *from European countries* may bring in the following items duty free: 200 cigarettes or 50 cigars or 250 gr. of tobacco; 2 liters of wine and 1 liter of spirits; 1 bottle toilet water (approx. 300 gr), 50 gr. of perfume. All other passengers (e.g., those from the U.S.) can bring in *twice* these amounts.

At the end of your stay you may take out up to $400 worth of goods (for real art objects you need an export permit). For goods of additional value, you can get export forms from the shop of purchase or from the Austrian National Bank in Vienna.

AUSTRIAN MONEY. The unit of Austrian currency is the Schilling, divided into 100 Groschen. In these days of inflation and fluctuating rates of exchange, you would be wise to check regularly on the dollar or sterling rates—both while planning your trip and while on it. A little forethought can save you money. At presstime (Spring '89), the rate of exchange was about AS13 to the U.S. dollar; the pound sterling was around AS22. The recent series of new banknotes has very little differentiation between the AS100 and AS500 notes; be careful, as confusion can be expensive.

Foreign currency and Austrian schillings (AS) may be brought into Austria in unlimited quantities. Any amount of foreign exchange may be taken out, plus AS100,000. Foreign currency may be exchanged at any Austrian bank and exchange offices at the following railway stations: Vienna Westbahnhof, and Süd-Ostbahnhof, Linz, Salzburg, Innsbruck, Kufstein, and Villach. Vienna airport also has a currency exchange office, and the exchange counter at the Reisebüro City on the Stephansplatz is open on Sundays. The 24-hour post offices also have counters where you can exchange money.

TIPPING. Almost all hotels (among the few exceptions are smaller country inns) now include service charges in their rates. For restaurants this includes 10% service and all the various taxes; it is nevertheless customary to tip about 5% of your bill. You tip the hotel concierge only for special services. Give the hotel porter AS10 per bag. When you take a taxi, no tip is included in the fare; 10% of the fare is the usual. If the driver has been helpful in other ways, give him 15%. The railway station porters charge AS10 a bag. Hat-check girls get AS7–15, depending on the locale. Washroom attendants get about AS5.

MAIL. Postage is about the same as in most European countries. For the first 20 grams (about ¼ ounce) letters cost AS5 for all domestic destinations; 6 for destinations abroad. Regular-size letters (20 grams) and postcards are forwarded within Europe automatically by airmail (with no extra charge); aerograms to U.S. and Canada AS11. Postcards to Austrian destinations 4, abroad 5, airmail postcards to U.S. and Canada 7.50. Have airmail letters weighed at the post office to be sure of correct postage.

Cables, telegrams, and wireless messages are sent from post offices. In addition to being available in post offices, stamps are sold in tobacco shops (Tabak Trafik) and it is often easier to buy them there, as post offices can get very busy.

TELEPHONES. Telephone numbers in Austria consist only of numerals (three to seven digits). Coin-operated street telephone booths in cities are numerous. Direct dialling everywhere within Austria as well as to most countries in the world; otherwise dial 09 for long-distance operator.

Calls within Austria are 33% cheaper between 6 P.M. and 8 A.M. on weekdays and from 1 P.M. on Saturday to 8 A.M. Monday. If you are calling Austria from abroad omit the "O" preceding the area code.

Major developments in the Austrian telephone system mean that numbers will be changing for years to come. We make every effort to keep numbers up to date, but check on the spot should you find it difficult to make your connection. This is particularly the case in Vienna and Innsbruck.

Warning—don't make long-distance calls from your hotel room without checking very carefully what the cost will be. Hotels frequently add several hundred percent to such calls. This is an international practice, not one confined to Austria alone. Go to the main post office or phone center for long-distance calls (in larger towns these are often open late or even round the clock). Alternatively, AT&T have a Teleplan service designed to overcome excessive surcharges. For details, call (in the U.S.) 800–874–4000. If you intend to use phone boxes a lot, buy a "Wertkarte" for AS95 at any post office. Wertkarte call boxes take the card rather than coins registering the time left on your card and give you AS100 worth in calls against the credit card.

CLOSING TIMES. Most stores open at 8.30 or 9 A.M. and close at noon or at 12.30 P.M. for a one- to two-hour lunch interval, and then stay open until 6 P.M.; in most villages opening time is 8 A.M. and lunch hour from

12 to 3 P.M. Some foodstores open at 7 A.M. and close at 6.30 P.M. with a two- to three-hour lunch break. At the Südbahn, Westbahn and Franz Josef stations, as well as in the 3rd District, Landstrasse 3, foodstores remain open till midnight.

Most of the stores in the city centers do not observe the lunch interval and stay open without interruption from 9 A.M. to 6 P.M. On Saturdays shops are open from 9 A.M. to noon. The usual office hours are 8 A.M. to 5 P.M., Sat. closed, except the first Saturday of the month, when most stay open until 5 or 6 P.M. Banking hours at main offices (larger banks) in Vienna are 8–3, branch offices 8–12.30; 1.30–3, Thurs. till 5.30 P.M., closed Sat. Note that banking hours vary from town to town. They are always closed on Saturdays. Most barbers and hairdressers close Monday.

National Holidays 1990. Jan. 1 (New Year's Day); Jan. 6 (Ephiphany); Apr. 15, 16 (Easter); May 1 (May Day); May 24 (Ascension); June 3, 4 (Whitsun); June 14 (Corpus Christi), Aug. 15 (Assumption); Oct. 26 (National Day); Nov. 1 (All Saints); Dec. 8 (Immaculate Conception); Dec. 25, 26 (Christmas).

Returning Home

CUSTOMS. U.S. Customs. You may bring in $400 worth of foreign merchandise as gifts or for personal use without having to pay duty, provided they have been out of the country more than 48 hours and provided they have not claimed a similar exemption within the previous 30 days. Every member of a family is entitled to the same exemption, regardless of age, and the exemptions can be pooled. For the next $1,000 worth of goods a flat 10% rate is assessed.

Included in the $400 allowance for travelers over the age of 21 are one liter of alcohol, 100 non-Cuban cigars and 200 cigarettes. Only one bottle of perfume trademarked in the U.S. may be brought in. However, there is no duty on antiques or art over 100 years old. You may not bring home meats, fruits, plants, soil or other agricultural products.

Gifts valued at under $50 may be mailed to friends or relatives at home, but not more than one per day of receipt to any one addressee. These gifts must not include perfumes costing more than $5, tobacco or liquor.

If you are traveling with such foreign-made articles as cameras, watches or binoculars that were purchased at home or on a previous trip, either carry the receipt or register them with U.S. Customs, using form 4457, prior to departure.

Canadian Customs. In addition to personal effects, and over and above the regular exemption of $300 per year, the following may be brought into Canada duty-free: a maximum of 50 cigars, 200 cigarettes, 2 pounds of tobacco and 40 ounces of liquor, provided these are declared in writing to customs on arrival. Canadian Customs regulations are strictly enforced; you are recommended to check what your allowances are and to make sure you have kept receipts for whatever you may have bought abroad. Small gifts can be mailed and should be marked "Unsolicited gift, (nature of gift), value under $40 in Canadian funds." For other details, ask for the Canada Customs brochure, *I Declare.*

British Customs. There are two levels of duty free allowance for people entering the U.K.: one, for goods bought outside the EEC or for goods bought in a duty free shop within the EEC; the other, for goods bought in an EEC country but not in a duty free shop.

In the first category you may import duty free: 200 cigarettes or 100 cigarillos or 50 cigars or 250 grammes of tobacco (*Note:* if you live outside Europe, these allowances are doubled); plus one liter of alcoholic drinks over 22% by volume (38.8% proof) or two liters of alcoholic drinks not over 22% by volume or fortified or sparkling wine, or two liters of table wine; plus two liters of table wine; plus 50 grammes of perfume; plus nine fluid ounces of toilet water; plus other goods to the value of £32.

In the second category you may import duty free: 300 cigarettes or 150 cigarillos or 75 cigars or 400 grammes of tobacco; plus 1½ liters of alcoholic drinks over 22% by volume (38.8% proof) or three liters of alcoholic drinks not over 22% by volume or fortified or sparkling wine, or three liters of table wine; plus five liters of table wine; plus 75 grammes of perfume; plus 13 fluid ounces of toilet water; plus other goods to the value of £250 (*Note* though it is not classified as an alcoholic drink by EEC countries for Customs' purposes and is thus considered part of the "other goods" allowance, you may not import more that 50 liters of beer).

In addition, *no animals or pets of any kind* may be brought into the U.K. The penalties for doing so are severe and are strictly enforced; there are *no* exceptions. Similarly, fresh meats, plants and vegetables, controlled drugs and firearms and ammunition may not be brought into the U.K. There are no restrictions on the import or export of British and foreign currencies.

Anyone planning to stay in the U.K. for more than six months should contact H.M. Customs and Excise, Kent House, Upper Ground, London S.E.1 (tel. 01–928 0533) for further information.

DUTY FREE. The duty free shops at the Austrian airports are run by Austrian Airlines, so prices are similar if not the same as those charged in the air. Vienna Airport has a reputation for being among the pricier of the European duty free shops, so look for local goods rather than the international brands. And VAT is charged, unless you point out that you are not a resident, or buy enough to qualify for a refund.

VIENNA

Splendors of the Past

by
RICHARD MOORE

Used as we are in the cities of the West to a life of instant shocks, endless crime, wall-to-wall noise and the rat-race rush all day long, Vienna comes as a relief. It is a city of civilized behavior, peaceful parks, elegant streets—a place where there is room to breathe. And yet, over the past five years, something of a rejuvenation has taken place. Bars, traffic-free zones, the UN, restoration of countless buildings, a lively avant-garde scene—all have played their part.

It is also a city that is more self-contained than most. According to the Tourist Board—in a fine moment of indiscreet candor—the population is "grumpy and cranky, arrogant and melancholy." But to the casual eye the Viennese are friendly, if reserved, welcoming and, above all, proud of their beloved old dowager of a town. In fact a high proportion of the Viennese themselves are middle-aged or elderly, which gives a sense of stability to the place. Crime is not the problem it is in many metropolitan centers, the streets are kept spotless and you can walk them safely at night. Mark you, the streets are mostly empty at night, although the city center is now lively with plenty on offer for all tastes until the small hours. Apart from the solid joys of the opera, operetta and concerts, among the finest in the world, Vienna has most to offer in the daytime, when you can absorb the

remaining echoes of a long and compelling history, enjoy some of the
world's greatest art, experience an ambience where music has been a way
of life for centuries, and come a little closer to the city where Beethoven
and Freud, Maria Theresa and Hitler, Mozart and Klimt all lived. You
will sense something of what Europe was like before the pulse of this century quickened to a beat that our grandfathers would never have understood.

The city in which this ambience exists is out of proportion to its modern
function. As we have said elsewhere, Austria is today merely the shrunken
remnant of a once mighty empire and Vienna was, above all, an imperial
city, built as a massive bureaucratic center housing all the offices and func-
tionaries that ordered the affairs of peoples throughout the emperor's vast
possessions. It was also the ceremonial center, with a network of palaces
that provided aristocratic shelter for the nobility who danced attendance
on the emperor when he was resident at either the Hofburg or Schönbrunn. While these magnificent buildings have mostly managed to find a
place in the modern state of things—frequently creating a bizarre juxtapo-
sition of Baroque glories and present stridency, as with the Museum of
Modern Art at the Palais Liechtenstein—the sheer number of them has
meant that the streets of Vienna are lined with magnificent monumental
doorways and the cliff-like march of stately facades. The city has been
stranded by its time-warp, left high and dry in the Europe of the 1980s,
and the miraculous thing is that the Viennese have succeeded in making
a virtue out of a necessity.

In fact, one of the most enjoyable aspects of a visit to Vienna is to see
just how the Viennese have managed to create a new, and completely valid,
way of life out of the shattered world of their past. This will manifest itself
to the visitor in a variety of ways, depending largely on personal interest.
The best possible equipment for getting the most out of the city is to have
a taste for history, a curiosity for the quirks in human nature, and a thirst
for art and music. A thirst for good wine comes in handy, too. In fact,
sitting in a 13th-century cellar, deep below the streets of Vienna, drinking
a goblet of crisp white wine, watching your fellow-drinkers and listening
to a quartet playing Mozart, would be difficult to beat as a typical Viennese
delight.

The Man That Hath not Music In His Soul . . .

Wherever you turn, you will find how deeply music is engrained in the
Viennese, indeed in all Austrians. Vienna has the most enormous variety
of musical events to offer, and events of an amazingly high standard. Performances by the Vienna Boys' Choir in the Hofburg Chapel on Sunday
mornings are events to remember. You will have an inkling of the world
of art that gave birth to Haydn and Schubert (both of whom were connected with the choir in their day) when you hear the purity and immediacy
of the boys' singing in its proper setting.

You will gain another insight into the way that music is looked upon
if you attend a performance at the Opera. Be careful to dress as formally
as you can while traveling, for opera is treated solemnly there, the intermissions becoming a kind of solemn processional rite. In the simple elegance of its reconstructed auditorium, with its ranked boxes, you will find
just as much intensity of attention as at the Metropolitan or Covent Garden, but somehow of a different quality, as if the audience were more ritu-

ally aware of participation in a theatrical tradition. For music in Vienna is a vital part of the great heritage of the city.

For yet another look at the importance of music in Vienna it is worth visiting the museum of musical instruments in the Hofburg complex. This is a collection of interest to the specialist as well as to the amateur. The pianos that were played by the great composers who graced Vienna's musical life, Beethoven, Brahms, Schumann and Schubert, are there. Pianos painted and carved, embellished with sphinxes and lyres, pianos that look like castles and pianos that look like cathedrals, even pianos that look like pianos.

Nor is the interest in keyboard instruments confined to pianos. That king of instruments, the organ, is well enthroned in Vienna. One of the finest organs in Vienna, and one that has been superbly rebuilt in recent years, is that of the Augustinerkirche. Every Friday in summer at 8 P.M. there is a concert given by international organists. It lasts an hour or so and is completely informal with a minimal charge on the door. The choral music here on Sundays and important church festivals is magnificent too.

The Importance of Serendipity

We mention elsewhere some of the dishes that will give you a taste of Vienna, but we cannot pass by the importance of dropping in to a coffeehouse at some point in your wanderings to sample the relaxed life of the city that goes on there. It is an ideal way of drinking coffee and atmosphere at the same time. The coffeehouse is the club, meeting place, gossip center and home-from-home for many Viennese. Coffee has a long and honorable history in the city. The Turks never managed to conquer Vienna, though, heaven knows, they tried hard enough. But they did leave one legacy, for the first beans to be used are believed to have been captured from the Turkish camp after the second siege was lifted. You will encounter innumerable coffeehouses as you wander round the streets of Vienna. At one time threatened, they have enjoyed a renaissance in recent years. Don't be shy of walking in, ordering a mokka and sitting quietly to enjoy the coming and going of the regulars.

Serendipity is very much a force in Vienna. One of the most unexpected and delightful sights is that to be seen on a bright day in late winter, when the touch of frost is still in the air, but the sun holds a promise of warmth. Then it is in, say, the grounds of the Belvedere, that you will see elderly Viennese, men and women, standing in the shelter of the palace wall, dressed in their sober clothes, with their faces to the sun, enjoying the respite from the winter's chill. Another is to see the troops of schoolchildren, brought from other parts of Austria to learn more of their nation's great heritage, weaving their way in orderly but excited lines through subways, museums and squares. It is a kind of microcosm of the way their mothers and fathers behave, for, though the Austrians are a formal, tidy, orderly people, they manage still to get a great deal of fun out of life.

An Eagle's-Eye View

Before exploring Vienna, it is a good idea to see it whole. No one can pretend that it is easy to climb the 345 steps of the south steeple of St. Stephen's Cathedral, but it is worth it as it affords a magnificent view right in the heart of town. For the less intrepid, there is an elevator to the top of the much lower north tower. The Big Wheel in the Prater affords one of the best and most readily accessible panorama views of Vienna, but the most romantic view is from the last projecting spur of the nearby mountains of the Vienna Woods.

Immediately below flows the Danube—not, unless you are phenomenally lucky, even remotely blue and too well-regulated to be romantic. Over a hundred years ago, a first artificial bed was cut to improve water transport and contain the spring floods which, however, still caused heavy damage when the snows melted abruptly. So a second channel through the broad inundation flats was completed in 1981, and the excavation soil was heaped into a 14-mile-long, 200-yard-wide island, used as a wild-life sanctuary and recreation area. This second bed, though mainly intended for water sports, also raised the groundwater level needed for Vienna's water supply in the extensive meadows round the Alte Donau (Old Danube). The latter is a cut-off branch of the River Danube forming a shallow (about 2-meters deep) lake some seven kilometers long and 300 to 500 yards wide. It is one of the favorite relaxation spots of the Viennese. The area is now a national park, its recreation area comprising the popular bathing beach of Gänsehäufel. The Winterhafen has been enlarged to deal with the increased water transport when the Rhine-Main-Danube canal has been completed.

The great city spreads across an extensive plain which continues over the Marchfeld toward the frontier of Czechoslovakia, marked by the rivers Thaya and March, less than 50 miles away. Upstream, to the left, lies the beautiful monastery of Klosterneuburg with its green-patina cupolas, on an eminence above the Danube.

A little higher up, on the opposite bank, is Korneuburg, with Kreuzenstein Castle atop a low hill. Behind Klosterneuburg rise the tree-clad heights of the Vienna Forest, coming to an end in the Lainzer Tiergarten, a natural wildlife preserve round the Empress Elisabeth's Hermes Villa, open to the public during the summer months. Below the wooded Tiergarten stands Maria Theresa's Baroque palace of Schönbrunn, with its formally laid-out gardens and the ornamental structure of the Gloriette behind. Through the flat country farther to the right the Danube flows on to Bratislava (Pressburg to the Austrians). From that city a spur of the Lower Carpathians runs off to the northeast.

Where the Danube flows through the gap between the Alps and the Carpathians across a broad basin, there Vienna grew up, astride the natural highway from the North Sea to the Adriatic. No political changes have been able to rob her of the importance she derives from this geographical position. Just south of Bratislava, some 65 km. (40 miles) from Vienna, begins the Hungarian Great Plain. Thus from these Viennese observation posts you are actually looking into two countries behind the Iron Curtain, both of which, of course, formed part of the Austro-Hungarian monarchy before World War I.

Legacy of Imperial Prosperity

Vienna does not really lie on the Danube; only the northern outskirts of the city touch it. The heart of Vienna, the Innere Stadt (Inner City) or First District—in medieval times, the entire city of Vienna—is bounded by the Ringstrasse (Ring) which forms almost a circle, with a narrow arc cut off by the Danube canal—dug in 1598—diverted from the main river just above Vienna and flowing through the city to rejoin the parent stream just below it. The Ring follows the lines of what, until an imperial decree ordered their leveling in 1857, were the defenses of the city—ramparts, moats and *glacis*. About 2 km. (just over a mile) beyond the Ring runs the roughly parallel line of the Gürtel, which until 1890 formed the outer fortifications, or Linienwall.

In the 1870's Vienna reached the zenith of its imperial prosperity. This was marked by such gigantic undertakings as the cutting of a new channel (with the overflow meadows) for the Danube, the building of the Great Exhibition of 1873, and the construction of the 90-km. water conduit from the natural underground reservoir in the Styrian mountains to the south of the city, which provides it with the most delicious ice-cold water to be found in any European capital.

This same prosperity found its expression in the series of magnificent buildings erected around the Ringstrasse when the fortifications were leveled—the Opera House, National Art Gallery, and National Museum of Natural History, the "New Wing" of the Hofburg, Parliament, the Rathaus, the University, and the Votivkirche. By the time the Gürtel took the place of the outer fortifications, there was not quite so much money available and, although many open spaces were laid out as parks, it has no noteworthy buildings.

Most of the older buildings are, naturally, to be found in the small area of the Inner City, including many Baroque palaces of the nobility. It was only after the invading Turkish hordes had been repulsed in 1683 that the area immediately beyond the Ring—the so-called "Inner Suburbs"—now numbered Bezirke (Districts) II to IX—began to develop, and the nobility to build summer residences here.

Of recent years many tall, functional, buildings have come to dominate the older, architecturally superior, districts. Notable among these is the United Nations City, situated in the Donau Park, overlooking the Danube. These high buildings, few in number by the standards of most modern cities, give an air of almost irrelevant modernity to a city whose heart beats with the pulse of history—meretricious costume jewelry around the neck of a dignified dowager.

A Crossroads Capital

Vienna is a triple capital. It is the capital of the Federal Republic of Austria and at the same time the capital city of two of the nine federal states that go to make up the country, Lower Austria and Vienna itself. Once the heart of an empire that reached across most of the known world, Vienna is now the chief city of a comparatively small nation and has a population of 1,580,600.

A glance at the map will show you that, though Vienna was once placed centrally in the heart of the Austro-Hungarian territories, since the modern partition of Eastern Europe it is now positioned in the extreme eastern tip of present day Austria. In fact it is less than 50 miles from the Iron Curtain and is actually further east than Prague. Vienna's geographical position and rich history both greatly influence, however subconsciously, what the visitor to the city sees and feels.

Vienna came into being at the point where two main routes of trade and tribal migration crossed. One of these highways was the Danube, a certain means of passage through an uncertain landscape, the other was the route from the Baltic down to the Adriatic. Its position sets it as a meeting ground, a place of parley between the lands to the west and the more oriental lands to the east. In fact the East can almost be said to begin at Vienna.

Where people had lived since the Stone Age there grew up a Celtic settlement, called Vindomina which, in turn, gave way to a Roman garrison, Vindobona. The Romans settled on this site in about 100 B.C., and it was intended to act as part of the fortifications to defend their eastern borders from attacks from the north. It was a big encampment—you can see just how big if you run your finger on the map following Rotgasse up from the Danube Canal, then Kramergasse, Graben into Naglergasse, turn down Tiefer Graben and back along Salzgries. These streets form almost the exact boundaries of Vindobona, and immediately you can see how Vienna's history is still written very clearly in the layout of her streets. To be able to trace a Roman fort 2,000 years later in the plan of a modern city is a delight for the history buff, and Vienna is hiding a lot of such delights. Of course, the early settlements were long before the days of the tamed Danube, and this small plateau rose above the turbulent waters of a frequently-flooding side branch of the great river. Nor was the establishing of this great camp the only act of the Romans which has survived. In these early centuries of the Christian era, the Romans planted vines along the nearby foothills, creating a tradition for wine-growing that has lasted. Not far from Vienna, at what is now Petronell, they built the capital of their province of Pannonia, Carnuntum, with two amphitheaters and all the solidity of a Roman provincial town.

After the Romans had pulled back to defend their heartland, a move completed by 488 A.D., the region became the prey of various Germanic tribes. It was in Vindobona that the *Nibelungenlied* sets the Whitsuntide wedding of Etzel (Attila) and Kriemhild, festivities that lasted for seventeen days with a crowd of guests so great that they could not all be lodged in the city. Which was hardly surprising, for in those days, only a century or so after the Romans had left, the place must have been just a ruined shell of its former self.

Babenbergs and Habsburgs

Tradition has it that Charlemagne visited the city at the end of the 8th century, a fairly safe bet, since he seems to have popped up all over Europe. The history of this period is a trifle unfocused and possibly includes the reign of a character called Samo, a mysterious Frankish merchant with twelve wives and forty-seven children. But the picture clears with the arrival of the Babenbergs. Margrave Leopold III became lord of Vienna in 1135, and the town was designated for the first time in documents as *civitas,* a city, in 1137. However, it was only under the first Duke, Heinrich Jasomirgott, that Vienna became the Austrian capital.

The Babenbergs were, by and large, a civilized clan, especially Leopold VI (1194–1230), under whom the Babenberg court in Vienna became a culturally brilliant center. The city expanded and, with Leopold the Glorious at the helm, defensive walls were finally fixed at the point where they would stay until they were demolished by Franz Josef in 1857.

If the Babenbergs began the expansion of Vienna, it was left to their successors, the Habsburgs, who took formal possession in 1278, to transform it over the next six and a half centuries into one of the great cities of the world. The history of the Habsburg dynasty and the history of Vienna became inextricably intertwined, and, as we explore the city, evidence of this interdependence will constantly appear. Not that, in the earlier days of the Habsburg dynasty, Vienna was the only city to have eminence; others, Graz, Linz and Innsbruck for example, even Prague, came to the fore from time to time, but in the end it was Vienna that won out.

To symbolize briefly the next few centuries—Vienna was afflicted with two great scourges, the Turks and the Plague. They were both deadly and both, also, were the cause of some of Vienna's greatest monuments, built in redemption of vows made in the direst moment of danger.

With the final defeat of the Turks in September 1683, Vienna could come out from behind her protecting, encircling walls, and was able to expand. After centuries of confinement within medieval boundaries, never knowing when the Turks would mount yet another siege, she was able to build once more in spreading safety.

This was the supreme period of Baroque Vienna, the years when the major buildings of the Hofburg, the Karlskirche (plague-inspired), the palaces of Schönbrunn and the Belvedere all appeared, along with many hardly lesser gems. With that strange promptness that often marks important periods in human affairs, native artists and architects, equipped to realize contemporary needs, were suddenly to hand. As if out of thin air Fischer von Erlach and Hildebrandt, Rottmayr, Troger and Daniel Gran materialized to embody the imperial spirit of an upsurging age in that singularly ebullient style, the Baroque. What forces were behind the sudden arrival of a totally indigenous, artistic powerhouse, capable not only of conceiving such huge works of art, but of successfully carrying them out, is one of those puzzles that will remain unanswered. But it is very clear that the challenge to recreate on Austrian soil imperial concepts as grandiose as Versailles and to provide settings fit for the triumphal Habsburgs, fuelled the inspiration of those artists chosen for the task.

The Baroque mold into which Vienna was cast, superseding the Gothic, is still very obvious as you walk around the Inner City, but subsequent ages also left their impression, especially the middle 1800s. It was in 1857 that the young Emperor Franz Josef commanded that the old circle of fortifications which had for so long acted as corset to the city—in fact, one of them was actually called Gürtel, Girdle—should be torn down; an act that gave the signal for the great surge of construction along the Ring. It was a really remarkable experiment in town planning, in many ways even more remarkable than the efforts of Baron Haussmann at exactly the same time in Paris. In a flurry of archeological enthusiasm and technical skill, buildings modeled on ancient Greece, Renaissance Italy and Gothic France began to rise along the new wide boulevards.

At the end of the 19th century another artistic wave broke over Vienna. Otto Wagner's buildings marked the city with the spirit of a new age. The Postsparkasse (Post Office Savings Bank, of all prosaic names for a great building this one has to win a prize) on Georg-Coch-Platz, is one of his finest, while the Secession building (Friedrichstrasse 12), designed by Joseph Olbrich with doors by Klimt, carried modernity a stage further with those touches of fantasy that characterize Jugendstil, the Austrian version of *art nouveau*.

Exploring Vienna

Before setting off around the city, a few general points. It is a good idea to plan your route for the day. Opening times of the major museums and other buildings you may wish to see are very variable, some open for a very short time only. The Prunksaal, for example, the main hall of the National Library, which is one of the glories of Vienna and indeed of the world, is open only from 11 to 12 in the morning from October to May, though during the rest of the year it is open from 10 to 4. Arriving at a museum you particularly wanted to see and finding that it shut half an hour before is intensely irritating, so it is wise to check up in advance. Among their many helpful pamphlets the Vienna Tourist Board have one giving the latest times when "Kultur" can be imbibed. We give some of the opening times in this book, but it is always as well to make sure they haven't changed.

Another extremely useful Tourist Board publication is called *Vienna from A to Z,* which currently costs 30 schillings. To explain. All the major buildings in the city have been equipped with small metal shields on their facades, shields which are decorated with flags in summer and which give basic information in German about the building. *Vienna from A to Z* is a catalog of these shields, in English, keyed to the number in a circle which is on all the shields. This excellent system has, in fact, turned the whole of the city into a wonderfully captioned art gallery.

Don't forget during your explorations that there are hundreds of cafes around the city which are ideal for rest, recuperation and the comfortable study of your guidebook. A half-hour spent over an icecream or a coffee will set you up for further forays and give you a breath of genuine Viennese life at the same time.

One last tip. Carry a lot of 10 schilling pieces with you. In most of the important churches and in many other buildings around town there are coin-operated tape machines that give you a commentary on the main points of interest in English and several other languages; all you have to do is press the right button.

The Opera

As good a place as any to start exploring the city is at the Opern-Passage, a large subterranean crossing under the Ring just by the Opera, that leads to the vast subway station extending as far as the Karlsplatz. While there is a tourist information office here where you can stock up on the various pamphlets and information with which to plan your trip, the main tourist office is now "upstairs," at Kärntnerstrasse 38, at the back of the Opera House, open 9–7 daily.

Above ground you will find the Opera House itself. It is a focus for Viennese life, and one of the chief symbols of resurgence after the cataclysm of World War II. The building was originally constructed in the middle of the 19th century, its first season being launched in 1869 with a performance of Mozart's *Don Giovanni.* In April 1945 it was almost totally destroyed, but the Viennese made it one of their first priorities when the hostilities ceased to rebuild their beloved Opera, restoring the auditorium, but incorporating many up-to-the-minute technical improvements in the stage region. The theater was reopened in November, 1955 and this time the chosen work was that great "resurrection" opera by another of Vienna's musical pantheon, Beethoven's *Fidelio.*

From September through June there are guided tours of the building every afternoon; five times daily in July and August. The auditorium is plain when compared with the red and gold eruptions of London's Covent Garden or some of the Italian opera houses, but it has an elegant individuality which shows to best advantage when the stage and auditorium together are turned into a ballroom for the great Opera Ball. The performances are sumptuous, with a lavish buffet in the intermissions and stately patrols through the fine long halls. If you secure a ticket you would be well advised to go sober-suited, otherwise you will feel rather out of place among the serious Viennese operagoers.

The affairs of the Opera House are of vital interest to the citizens of Vienna. Even those who never darken the Opera's doors read about the doings of the administration—artistic and financial—with avidity, as a long line of directors have had good cause to know. The problem is one that seems extremely odd to the outside world, for the position of Director is virtually the top job in Austria, almost as important as that of President, and one that comes in for even more public attention. Every man-on-the-street thinks he could do it just as well and, since the huge salary comes out of the taxes, he feels that he has every right to criticize, often and loudly. Vienna is a city where opera is taken very, very seriously.

Grouped around the Opera are several famous haunts, the Hotel Bristol, the Café Mozart and, most renowned, Sacher's. Sacher's is firmly ensconced in Viennese legend and, of course, the home of the celebrated chocolate cake, the Sachertorte, about which there raged a famous law suit over who precisely could lay claim to being the makers of the cake. Sachertorte, as opposed to Sacher Torte, is now only made by Sacher's!

When you cross the road behind the Opera to reach the pedestrian zone of the Kärntnerstrasse, you will be introduced to one of the basic facts of Viennese life. One does not jaywalk. You will see throngs of people patiently waiting at pedestrian crossings for the lights to change, even when the street is totally and completely clear of traffic, with apparently nothing in sight as far as the Wienerwald.

Kärntnerstrasse

Stretching ahead from the back righthand corner of the Opera is Kärntnerstrasse and the beginning of a pedestrian precinct that runs through the heart of Vienna's Inner City shopping area. It has openair cafés down the middle in summer and is generally attractive to wander through and to window shop. The Viennese hotly dispute if the introduction of this pedestrian mall has changed one of Europe's smartest shopping streets for the better.

On your left at number 38 is the *Vienna Information* office. A little further down on the right, tucked between shops, is the restored facade of the Malteserkirche, Church of the Knights of Malta, one of the few Orders remaining from the days of the Crusades. The interior is Gothic and some 600 years old, its plain walls decorated with plaques bearing the arms of the Grand Masters of the Order. The present Order is recognized diplomatically in about 40 countries, it numbers some 3,000 members around

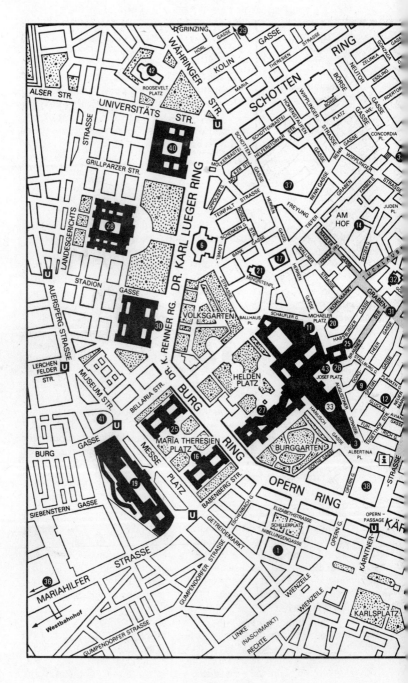

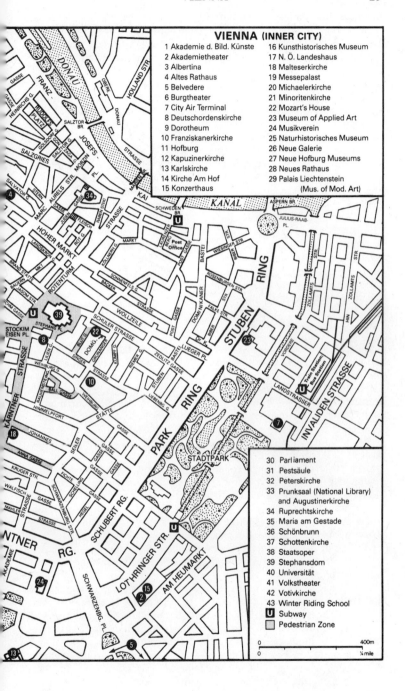

VIENNA (INNER CITY)

1 Akademie d. Bild. Künste
2 Akademietheater
3 Albertina
4 Altes Rathaus
5 Belvedere
6 Burgtheater
7 City Air Terminal
8 Deutschordenskirche
9 Dorotheum
10 Franziskanerkirche
11 Hofburg
12 Kapuzinerkirche
13 Karlskirche
14 Kirche Am Hof
15 Konzerthaus
16 Kunsthistorisches Museum
17 N. Ö. Landeshaus
18 Malteserkirche
19 Messepalast
20 Michaelerkirche
21 Minoritenkirche
22 Mozart's House
23 Museum of Applied Art
24 Musikverein
25 Naturhistorisches Museum
26 Neue Galerie
27 Neue Hofburg Museums
28 Neues Rathaus
29 Palais Liechtenstein
   (Mus. of Mod. Art)

30 Parliament
31 Pestsäule
32 Peterskirche
33 Prunksaal (National Library) and Augustinerkirche
34 Ruprechtskirche
35 Maria am Gestade
36 Schönbrunn
37 Schottenkirche
38 Staatsoper
39 Stephansdom
40 Universität
41 Volkstheater
42 Votivkirche
43 Winter Riding School
U Subway
Pedestrian Zone

0 400m
0 ¼ mile

the world and the present Grand Master is, technically at least, a Head of State. It is, in fact, one of the biggest and one of the least known charitable organizations in the world today.

One of the delights of wandering around Vienna is to be able to compare the architecture and atmosphere of the city's many churches. Around a dozen will appear in the following pages and that in no way exhausts the possibilities. It is interesting to trace the changing styles over the centuries from the simple, almost severe interiors of churches such as this one, to the enormously elaborate Baroque decorations of those built (or at least ornamented) in the early 18th century.

The narrow sidestreets to the right of Kärntnerstrasse contain a wealth of Baroque palaces and houses including (back, before the Malteserkirche) the 17th-century Annakirche decorated by Daniel Gran; the Kremsmünster Court in Annagasse; the Baroque wing of the Hofkammerarchiv (Imperial Household Records Office) which backs on to the simpler 19th-century wing in the Johannesgasse, next to the 17th-century Ursulinenkirche. The Ministry of Finance's offices are housed in a masterpiece of the Baroque, Prince Eugene of Savoy's Winterpalace, designed by Fischer von Erlach—the staircase, with sculptures by Giovanni Guiliani, is breathtaking—and extended by Lukas von Hildebrandt, who likewise inspired the former Monastery Zur Himmelpforte (At the Gate of Heaven) after which the street is named.

The Imperial Vault

Back on Kärntnerstrasse, a few yards past the Malteserkirche but on the left, is a short turning that leads directly into the Neuer Markt. On the left of this square, opposite, is the Kapuzinerkirche (Church of the Capuchins), again at least 600 years old. The plain facade has been restored to its original 17th-century design, while the simple white interior sets off the warm browns of the marquetry work behind the high and side altars.

Below this church lie the bodies of the imperial house of Austria in the Kaisergruft, the Imperial Vault. Perhaps this is the wrong way to approach the Habsburgs in Vienna for the first time, starting with their tombs, but it does give you a chance to get their names in sequence as they lie in their serried ranks, their coffers ranging from the simplest through positive explosions of funerary conceit with decorations of skulls and other morbid symbols to the lovely and distinguished tomb of Maria Theresa and her husband, designed while the couple still lived. To pass by these long lines of imperial dead is to take a short journey through history and art, and impresses one with a sense of exactly how the Habsburg centuries unfolded.

The Capuchin monks guide the groups of visitors among the tombs of 138 Habsburgs, from Ferdinand II in 1633 to Franz Josef in 1916. The Countess Fuchs was the only non-royal to be buried here—a well-deserved honor for this dearly-loved surrogate mother to the children of Maria Theresa. The Countess was the Empress's own governess to begin with, and without her Maria Theresa would never have been able to conduct affairs of state *and* raise a family. Only one coffin was ever taken away. In 1940, after Germany defeated France, the remains of the Duke of Reichstadt, the son of Napoleon and Marie Louise, were transferred to Les Invalides in Paris upon the personal order of Adolf Hitler, who was hoping to appease the French with the gesture. Zita, widow of Austria's last Kaiser, Carl, was buried here in 1989, doubtless the last of the Habsburgs to find a final resting place here.

In the center of the Neuer Markt is the Baroque Donner Brunnen, the Providence Fountain, the work of Georg Raphael Donner, one of the leading 18th-century artists of Vienna. The original lead figures are in the Baroque Museum in the Lower Belvedere—and, one has to admit, look better there than the copies do here. Providence stands in the middle and the four figures at the corners represent four Austrian rivers, the Traun, Enns, Ybbs and March. These four figures are among Donner's most attractive works; the poise of the young man with the trident, leaning over the basin, is particularly lifelike, although his accessible pose leaves him open to easy indignities.

Further along Kärntnerstrasse a turning on the right, Weihburggasse, leads past the hotel Kaiserin Elisabeth, where many famous people have stayed over the decades, Wagner and Liszt among them. On the other side of the street is a famous restaurant, the Drei Husaren (Three Hussars) which, although one of Vienna's fanciest and most expensive, you might want to return to one evening. Further along in the next block is the excellent British Bookshop where you can stock up on reading material (and don't be put off by the closed door, it's almost certainly open for business).

Franziskanerplatz is a charming, small square, with a fountain topped off by an exceptionally urbane Moses in the middle. To one side is the former residence of Countess Fuchs, governess of Maria Theresa. It has been restored to its extremely elegant former looks. On the facade of the Gothic-Renaissance Franziskanerkirche (Franciscan Church) is a statue of St. Jerome, lion in attendance and golden cardinal's hat on his head. The interior of this church is a cheerful one, with a most dramatically conceived backing to the altar, containing a painting of *The Immaculate Conception* by Rottmayr.

Kärntnerstrasse opens into Stephansplatz at Stock-im-Eisen (Trunk-in-Iron), a treetrunk into which every 16th-century apprentice blacksmith drove a nail before leaving Vienna. You can still see this odd relic preserved in a glass case up on the wall on a left-hand corner. Hans Hollein's new "Haas Haus" on the corner of Graben and Stock-im-Eisen Platz should be finished by 1990 and promises to provide a controversial talking point, as did the Loos House on Michaelerplatz at the turn of the century (see p. 105).

St. Stephen's Cathedral

Stephansdom (St. Stephen's Cathedral) is another focus for the pride of the Viennese in their city. It shared with the Opera and some other major buildings the fate of having been very heavily damaged in World War II, and of having risen from the fires of destruction like a phoenix. And like the phoenix, it is a symbol of regeneration.

Now that the work on the subway is finished—in this part of the city at least—it is possible to prowl around the cathedral to your heart's content, without being sent flying by raucous traffic. It sits in the middle of a wide piazza, the space round it seeming larger than it actually is. To one side of the great building, close to where Kärntnerstrasse meets the square, you will see the outlines of two buildings superimposed on each other in colored stone on the paving. Two chapels used to stand here, one dedicated to Mary Magdalene and the other to St. Virgilius. The deep delving for the subway, which went right up to the foundations of the cathedral, revealed not only some Roman remains and lots of bones, for the area had once been a graveyard, but also the Virgilkappelle almost complete, as it had been when encased in the crypt of the Maria Magdalena Kappelle. It is now cocooned in the subway ticket hall below Stephansplatz and can be visited. It is a severe vaulted chamber which seems like part of the catacombs. As you go in there is a small collection of pottery from different periods found around the city during various excavations. If the chapel is closed, you can look down into it through a large window in the ticket hall.

A first St. Stephen's was built by Duke Heinrich Jasomirgott in 1147 and, following a fire, replaced by a Romanesque basilica during the reign of King Ottocar of Bohemia. The Great West Front thus dates from the late 13th century, with the soaring Riesentor (Giant Doorway) flanked by two small towers (Heidentürme) on either side. There are a lot of attractive details in the carving here, Samson wrenching open the lion's jaws, a griffin, and all sorts of mythical beasts.

Continuing round to the left, you will pass by the unfinished north tower—unfinished, that is, when compared with its brother on the south side. It was decided not to rival the sky-piercing south spire and to leave the north tower a mere stump, called the Adlerturm. Inside is one of Vienna's traditional treasures, Die Pummerin, the Boomer; a huge bell weighing around 22 tons and measuring 10 feet across. The original Boomer was cast in 1711 from cannon captured from the Turks. In the south tower until 1945, it crashed down into the nave during a fire and was replaced in 1952, in the north tower. The new Boomer was carried in solemn procession from St. Florian in Upper Austria, where it had been cast as part of Upper Austria's contribution to the rebuilding and refurnishing of St. Stephen's. You can visit the bell by an elevator.

The northwest door is another masterpiece of medieval work. As it used to be the women's entrance to the cathedral (the southwest door was for men only) it features mainly female saints and incidents from the life of the Virgin.

Next on the circumambulation comes the openair pulpit named after the monk Capistranus who, in 1450, preached from it to rouse the people of the city to a crusade against the Turks. The elaborate group above the simple pulpit was added in 1737 and shows the saint (he was canonized in 1690) spearing a symbolic Turk to a flourish of flags and cherubs. Close by this spot the body of Mozart rested briefly in 1791 on the way to his burial. He died not far away in a house on Rauhensteingasse (Number 8, although the original house is no longer there).

Further round the east side of the cathedral is the torso of the Man of Sorrows which is irreverently known as *Our Lord of the Toothache,* because of its agonized expression. Nearby are more carvings, especially a 1502 scene of the events on the Mount of Olives.

You are now at the base of Alte Steffl, Old Steve, the dominating feature of the Vienna skyline. It is 450 feet high and was built between 1359 and 1433. If you feel fit enough, you can climb the 345 steps to take advantage of the stupendous view from the top of the tower section, not of the spire itself, of course. From that vantage point you can see out over the city to the rising slopes of the Wienerwald.

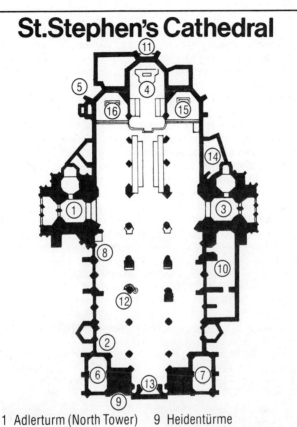

St.Stephen's Cathedral

1 Adlerturm (North Tower)
2 Altar Canopy by Hans
   Puchspaum
3 Alte Steffl (Belfry)
4 Baroque High Altar
5 Capistranus Pulpit
6 Chapel of the Cross
7 Chapel of Elgius
8 Elevator to Pummerin;
   Entrance to Catacombs
9 Heidentürme
10 New Sacristy
11 "Our Lord of the Toothache"
12 Pulpit by Anton Pilgram
13 Riesentor (Giant
    Doorway)
14 Sexton's House
    (Entrance to Alte Steffl)
15 Tomb of Frederick III
16 Wiener Neustadt Altar

To the right of the southwest door stands the statue of Duke Rudolf IV, who ordered the Gothic enlargement of the cathedral, holding a model of the building in his right hand. Both he and his wife, Katharine, who balances him on the other side of the door, are attended by heralds carrying their coats of arms. The arch continues upwards with statues of saints, while four scenes from the life of St. Paul fill in the tympanum.

Inside the cathedral there are many easily identifiable things to see and a great deal of atmosphere to absorb. The fabric was extensively rebuilt after the terrible damage of 1945 when the cathedral was caught in the crossfire of the two locked armies, and suffered not only gunfire but block-busters and incendiary bombs into the bargain. It is difficult now, sitting quietly, drinking in the shadowed peace, to tell what was original and what parts of the walls and valuting were reconstructed. One of the things that has helped towards this merging of the new with the old is that many of the treasures of medieval carving were rescued. Among these is the pulpit sculptured by Anton Pilgram between 1510 and 1515, with the vivid heads of the early Fathers of the Church, Augustine, Gregory, Jerome and Ambrose, and with Pilgram's own carved face peering out from behind a shutter under the stairs. All the way up the intricate balustrade are delightful animals symbolizing sins.

There is another self-portrait bust of Pilgram under the organ support, like a huge bracket, on the wall of the north side. This one dates from the same time as the pulpit (1513) and is a masterpiece of early portraiture, closely akin to the work of Dürer, who was a contemporary.

The Apostelchor (Apostles' Choir), the south choir, contains the tomb of Frederick III, another masterpiece, this time the work of Nikolaus of Leyden who took 45 years to complete it, from 1467 to 1513. With carvings representing Good and Evil (protective spirits and animals) all round, the monumental marble block on top depicts the emperor in his coronation robes.

The Marienchor (Virgin's Choir) contains the tomb of Rudolph IV, the founder of both the cathedral and of Vienna University whose small statue was on the southwest door. Apart from some lovely medieval figures on the wall here, the thing that draws the eye is the Wiener Neustadt altar which dates from 1447. A riot of wood carving, gilt and color, it was brought to St. Stephen's from the Cistercian Monastery of Wiener Neudstadt in 1884. It represents the three figures of the Virgin and the saints Barbara and Catherine, with the Coronation of the Virgin above and scenes from her life in the wings. Resting on the top of this reredos are the remains of an altarpiece dedicated to St. Andrew (c. 1420).

The central, early Baroque, high altar (1647) is a turmoil of black marble with a picture of the cathedral's patron saint being stoned to death.

There is much else to see; the Catacombs, where the internal organs of the Habsburgs rest, all except their hearts (one has the impression that the Day of Resurrection is going to be an extremely busy one among the various crypts of Vienna while the Habsburgs pull themselves together); in the Catacombs can be seen the vestiges of the original basilica which was burned down in 1258, thus opening the way for the construction of the present building; the Eligius Chapel, to the right of the main entrace, with some exquisite sculpture, especially the statue of St. Ludmilla with her palm leaf, and a Virgin and child; and the Kreuzkappelle (Chapel of the Cross), on the other side of the west door, and a Baroque wrought-iron grille and the tomb of Prince Eugene of Savoy.

On one of the pillars of the nave is a stone plaque telling of the various contributions of other parts of the country to the reconstruction. Each province took responsibility for a particular section of the work. There may be other church interiors which have more striking architectural features, but there are very few that represent the investment of more civic pride than does St. Stephen's. The interior has now finally been cleaned and repainted.

Teutonic Knights and Mozart

Under the very shadow of the cathedral is the Deutschordenskirche (Church of the Teutonic Knights), at Singerstrasse 7. The church is small and deceptively simple, dating back to the middle of the 14th century. It is a perfectly maintained, white interior with the arms of the past Masters on the walls.

The Baltic area was the realm of the Order in the Middle Ages—and realm is not too strong a word, for although the High Master of the Order was not actually a king, he was an unchallenged monarch. At the height of their power in the 14th century, the Teutonic Knights tried to build a Kingdom of God on earth in the lands bordering the Baltic—Danzig, East Prussia, Livonia and Estonia. With military dictatorship, theocracy and colonialism all working in a strange unison, the Knights forged a history that is too little known. A relic from the Order's days in the Baltic is the 16th-century winged altarpiece, painted in the Netherlands and once housed in St. Mary's Church in Danzig. It was moved to its present position in 1808. Sadly, it is not easy to see this lovely work without help, as it is set back on the altar.

On the second floor above the church is the Treasury of the Order. Usually under the guardianship of a brother of the Order is a multifarious collection of items from the Order's long history. Coins and documents, especially a charter of Henry IV of England, with a fine seal; silver and gold table decorations of fine craftsmanship—a salt cellar decorated with "adders tongues", actually fossilized teeth which were supposed to detect poison in food; a stag with antlers and earrings of coral; a complicated astronomical clock, with jewels and filigree work; weapons and ceremonial dress; medieval paintings. From the window of the last room, the one that contains the paintings, there is a fine view down into the beautifully-kept courtyard of the building, dominated by the soaring presence of the cathedral.

Continue a little way down Singerstrasse, turn into Blutgasse and then right into Domgasse. Here, at Number 5, Mozart lived from 1784–87 and composed *The Marriage of Figaro*. It is now a commemorative museum. In the block formed by Domgasse, Blutgasse, Singerstrasse and Grünangergasse there is a grouping of old houses, called Fähnrichshof, that has been restored.

Much restoration of facades has taken place in Vienna. Many buildings have been washed and countless houses have had their frontages repainted. The face of old Vienna is much brighter than for many long years.

A Basilisk and the Old University

The Viennese are essentially apartment dwellers, but apartment dwellers with a difference. Their apartments are inward looking. The whole of the old city consists of high buildings, some with very thick ancient walls, built round central courtyards. These "castles" close up tight in the evening as the citizens pull up their metaphorical drawbridges and prepare for the night's siege. In the daytime one can peek into some of these inner courtyards to see the great variety of architecture they represent, but remember that they are integral parts of private houses, so peek politely.

Across Stephansplatz from the North Tower of the cathedral is the 17th-century Archiepiscopal Palace which houses the very interesting Diocesan Museum. A small lane runs through the buildings here down to Wollzeile, named after the wool merchants and weavers who once lived and worked in the neighborhood.

The next street parallel to Wollzeile, Bäckerstrasse (starting at the small square, Am Lugeck, where there is a statue of the inventor of printing, Gutenberg) has many historic houses, Number 14 being especially interesting with a Renaissance courtyard, dating from the end of the 16th century. Keep your eye roving over the facades as you walk along; you will surprise all sorts of carving and other decorations.

Sonnenfelsgasse, the next down on the left, also has many lovely houses, especially Number 15, with a fine gateway. This is now the area of the Old University. The square, Dr. Ignaz-Seipel-Platz (also known as Universitätsplatz) is named after one of the first Chancellors of the Austrian Republic, who lived from 1876–1932 and was not only a politician but also a Catholic priest and expert on international law, an unusual combination. He was enormously influential in forming modern Austria and steered his country through the chaos of the 1920s, maintaining a simplicity of life that unnerved some of his staff. He would travel to international meetings by third-class railway carriage.

The 1627 facade of the University Church of the Assumption (Jesuitenkirche) takes up one side of the narrow square. It was originally built in the early 17th century, but was given its present sumptuously ornate interior by the architect Andrea Pozzo between 1703 and 1705. An abbé, Pozzo was also a great fresco painter and he brought his talent to the ethereal ceilings here, as well as to the twisting columns and the dramatic altar with its high-flying crown.

Down one of the other sides of the square is the great Ceremonial Hall of the Old University (now called the Akademie der Wissenschaften—Academy of the Sciences) built in the 1750s by a French architect, Jean-Nicolas Jadot de Ville-Issey, a court architect to Maria Theresa. It is very much a neo-classical building and clearly the work of an artist working in the disciplines of French symmetry. The opposite side of the square is taken up by the Alte Universität, where the original University was housed, ruled by the Jesuits. This building is from 1623–27. Careful cleaning is restoring to this small square a large measure of its original elegance and color; indeed the whole complex is to be renovated over the next five years.

Curving round behind the University Church is Schönlaterngasse (Street of the Beautiful Lantern), once part of Vienna's medieval *Quartier Latin* and rapidly becoming so again. Attractive bars, literary cafes, galleries and boutiques are creating a lively atmosphere, very much to the students' taste and intriguing to visitors.

Number 7 is the Basiliskenhaus, one of the earliest houses in the area, parts of it dating from as early as 1212. In those days the house was a bakery and a basilisk, a small fire-breathing and very deadly type of dragon, was living in the well, poisoning the water and turning anyone who came near to stone. A young baker's apprentice, clearly well versed in the classical myths, managed to kill the unpleasant lodger by showing it a mirror and so turning it to stone, in its turn.

Just along from the Basilisk House is Alte Schmiede (The Old Smithy), a commercially run place containing a reconstruction of a medieval blacksmith's workshop, with a restaurant and art gallery.

On the other side of the Basilisk House is an arched gateway leading into the quiet close of the Heiligenkreuzerhof. This was once the city residence of the Cistercian monks from Heiligenkreuz (Holy Cross), which lies not so many miles from Vienna, close to Mayerling. Many of the great monastic foundations of the Middle Ages had their urban headquarters, in much the same way as the great families maintained a city palace so as to be near the corridors of power, and this was one such. The small square, really a large courtyard, contains a lovely Baroque chapel of St. Bernard; unfortunately, rarely open.

Schönlaterngasse leads to the main Post Office next to the church of the Dominicans, after whom a remaining bastion of the old fortifications is named. The regular postal counters and all-night post office facilities are in the building to the left, in the Fleischmarkt.

Adjoining Rotenturmstrasse is Fleischmarkt, since at least 1285 the center of the meat trade, the butcher's quarter, but also meeting place of the Greek merchants, a fact still commemorated in the names Griechengasse and Griechenbeisl (Greek Tavern), the latter an atmospheric old restaurant. The Greek church, next to the Griechenbeisl on the Fleischmarkt, has been cleaned and restored and is now a magnificent fantasia of brick and gold leaf. Part of the ancient city defenses can be seen here at Number 9 (a 13th-century tower, best viewed from the courtyard of Number 7). Number 9 Fleischmarkt has an attractive 16th-century sculpture of the Virgin on its facade.

St. Rupert and the Romans

Just above the point where Fleischmarkt intersects Rotenturmstrasse, lies Hohe Markt. This square is notable as the place where you can see part of the Roman foundations that have been unearthed, for this was roughly the middle of the Roman encampment. In the basement of No. 3 there is a small museum, with sections of two Roman houses which were revealed during drainage work in 1948. Further excavations have made this quite an interesting place to visit, with the Roman central heating (hypocaust) and other remains, as well as excellent maps of the area.

The square as a whole has had a lot of restoration. In the middle is a lovely fountain, now renovated and almost rivaling the Plague Column for interest. It is called the Vermählungsbrunnen (the Fountain of the Virgin's Wedding) and it dates from 1732. High on an arch in one corner of the square is the Anker Clock, a delightful 1911 confection, with many Viennese figures marking the time—among them Marcus Aurelius, and Haydn. Midday is the time to see the full procession in all its splendor. There is a plaque on the wall to the left of the clock which carries details of the figures.

Rotenturmstrasse slopes down from the cathedral to the Danube Canal at Franz Josefs Kai. "Kai" is the same word as "quay," and this was the stretch of the bank where, in the old days, the fishing boats and the merchants' vessels tied up. Turn left, and two blocks along you will come to the Church of St. Rupert (Ruprechtskirche) standing high above the embankment. On street level is the site of the hotel which, during World War II, was the Gestapo headquarters, demolished in postwar disgust. There is a prominent commemoration stone in its place.

St. Rupert's is an old church, parts being from the 11th century, but it was almost certainly built on the site of a gateway of Vindobona, and no doubt some of the Roman masonry was used in the first foundations, laid, so legend says, around 740. St. Rupert was the patron saint of the Danubian salt merchants, and you will notice the carved bucket that accompanies his statue outside the church. The building is often locked, indeed you may only get in by going to a service on Sunday. The nave and tower are pure, simple Romanesque, and the remainder Gothic. There are some attractive modern decorations, including some very contemporary windows in yellow and blue, which harmonize surprisingly well with the ancient stones.

This, then, is the heart of the Roman settlement. A little beyond St. Rupert's is another memory of those early days in the name of the street that runs up from Franz Josefs Kai—Marc Aurelstrasse, called after the Roman philosopher-emperor. Walk up this sloping street (it has no particular points of interest) and along its continuation, Tuchlauben, and then turn right down Bognerstrasse, you will reach . . .

Am Hof

Am Hof is yet another impressive square. In the center stands the Mariensäule (Virgin's Column), erected originally in 1646 after the delivery of the city from the Swedes during the Thirty Years' War. That column was removed and the present one put up in 1667. Around the base are the figures of War, Hunger, Plague and Heresy, all very real dangers during so many of Vienna's long centuries.

Am Hof is so called from the fact that the Babenbergs had their palace (castle might be a better word) here, before the center of power was moved under the Habsburgs to the Hofburg. The site of this court was to one side of the square, where Number 7 now stands. It was, naturally, the scene of intriguing events in medieval times. Vienna was on the route to the Holy Land, and many crusaders, among them Barbarossa, stayed here. Walter von der Vogelweide, the famous Minnesinger who features in Wagner's *Tannhäuser,* was a figure of the Babenberg court in the 1190s when it was a center for art and poetry.

On the opposite side of Am Hof is the Church of the Nine Choirs of Angels, the Kirche Am Hof. The facade is a wonderful example of the early Baroque style, designed by Carlo Carlone in 1662. From the deep central balcony Pope Pius VI blessed the city in 1782 and, on August 6th, 1806 heralds proclaimed the end of the Holy Roman Empire of the German Nation. This facade, with its windows, statues and recessed wings, is more like the varied front of a palace than of a church. The interior seems simpler than it is, with its octagonal pillars, grey and white coloring and very high ceiling. The generally subdued effect provides a muted background for the paintings, and of these the finest is probably the ceiling fresco by Maulpertsch, in one of the side chapels to the left.

Back in the square, notice the attractive house, Number 38, painted in tones of ocher, a simple yet very pleasing facade. Number 83 has an interesting sculpture of the Virgin. In the corner of the square is a facade that is anything but simple, it is an ornate building which looks as if it started life as a triumphal arch and carried on from there. You will be surprised to find that it is the headquarters of the Fire Brigade but, to be fair, it was once the City Armory, was "Baroqued" in the early 1730s and is surely the most unlikely fire house to be found anywhere.

In the tiny streets behind the church, Schulhof and Seitzergasse, you can see the Gothic walls of the choir. You will find a fine old restaurant, the Gösser Bierklinik (Steindlgasse 4) nearby. We enjoy the way they cook game in season so much that we have never dared find out just what a "Beer Clinic" might be. Around the corner, at Schulhof 2, is the Uhren-museum (Clock Museum), containing over 3,000 timepieces of every description, from the 1440s to today's electronic marvels. The prize exhibit is an astronomical clock of 1769 by Rutschmann.

Take Parisergasse into Judenplatz where there is a rather clumsy statue of the German dramatist Lessing. This was the medieval ghetto of Vienna and must have witnessed many scenes of human misery. The plight of the Jews in the days before the Enlightenment was not a happy one. In 1421 two hundred and ten were burned alive, and for the next two centuries Jews were constantly humiliated. It is a part of Viennese history that should be remembered today with pain.

There are interesting houses here, in and around the Judenplatz. Number 4 is another Mozart House; at the corner of the square, on Number 12 Kurrentgasse, two pillars support a flying lion and a fish; Number 2 has an attractive Gothic bas relief; and Number 11, which continues through to become Wipplingerstrasse 7, is the former Bohemian Court Chancery, built by Johann Bernhard Fischer von Erlach from 1708 to 1714, though changed later. Walk around this building into Wipplinger-strasse and there you will see two really superb frontages facing each other across the street. The front of the Bohemian Chancellery is the original Fischer von Erlach one, with sculptures by Mattielli, and what sculptures they are! Across the road, its statues protected from the pigeons by netting, is the Alte Rathaus, the Old Town Hall. It had been the Guildhall for centuries before it received its lovely facade in 1699.

Go through one of the short, arched passages into the Alte Rathaus' central courtyard. Against one wall is the Andromeda Fountain, by Georg Raphael Donner. This is a gentle work of bas relief, with Andromeda (whom legend says was an Ethiope, though she certainly isn't in this version) and the dragon in the foreground, and with Perseus about to swoop down for the kill. The work is normally dated 1741, but since Donner died in the February of that year, it must almost certainly be placed a little earlier.

From another corner of the courtyard an archway leads to Salvator-gasse. Turn left and walk a short way along to the Church of Maria am Gestade.

St. Mary on the Banks (Maria am Gestade) is one of the finest Gothic churches in Vienna. It used to stand on the edge of the river, as its name shows, but it is now quite a bit inland from the water. It was built on Roman foundations and also on a 12th-century church, which accounts for the rather strangely angled nature of the floor plan of the present building. The inside has just been restored to reveal much previously unsuspected beauty. The church as it now stands is late 14th century though restored after the damage caused during the Turkish sieges. The tower is seven-sided and culminates in a lacey crown. Inside, the feeling of the nave is pure unadulterated Gothic (it is worth comparing this church with the mock-Gothic of the Votivkirche). In a small chapel to the right, halfway up the nave, are two superb parts of a triptych by the Master of Maria Stiegen (1460); they show the *Annunciation* and the *Coronation of the Virgin* and are of a quality rarely seen in public outside the most prestigious galleries. Also worth remarking are the figures high up around the nave and some of the stained glass.

St. Peter's Church

Leading out of Stephansplatz is the Graben, another attractive shopping street and part of the widespread central pedestrian mall. The Pestsäule (Plague Column) shoots up from the middle of the Graben like a geyser of whipped cream. It was erected between 1682 and 1693 to commemorate the deliverance of Vienna from the Black Death which had raged in the city in 1679. A huge number died and the Emperor Leopold I vowed this memorial while the plague still held sway. Among the sculptors who worked on the column was Johann Bernhard Fischer von Erlach whom, with his son, we will meet constantly around Vienna. It is worth surmounting the overall effect of swirling upward movement to look more closely at many of the excellently sculpted details. This is one of the most exuberant Baroque monuments anywhere (especially in its cleaned and regilded state) and as such deserves close inspection.

Just past the column, on the right, is a short turning leading to Peterskirche (St. Peter's Church). Mind the traffic; frustrated by not getting into the Graben it's fairly fierce. St. Peter's was built at the very beginning of the 18th century, but the site had held several churches before that. There is a panel on the outside showing the first Christian temple in Vienna being founded by Charlemagne, a quite possible legend. True or not, the site was long hallowed by the time the present structure was begun. It was finished by the middle 1730s and so is exactly contemporary with the more imperial Karlskirche.

The main architect was Johann Lukas von Hildebrandt and the interior is probaby the best example of church Baroque in Vienna, certainly the most theatrical. The fresco on the dome is by Rottmayr but is a bit difficult to see clearly unless the light is coming from the right angle. It shows the *Coronation of the Virgin,* a favorite subject for ceilings as it calls for an imitation sky with lots of clouds and flying angels. The pulpit is an especially fine one with a highly ornate canopy and opposite the pulpit is what can only be described as a religious tableau. Its subject is the martyrdom of St. John Nepomuk, who was thrown into the River Moldau, and here, like a scene on stage are the gold figures of the saint and his brutal attackers and the silver waters of the river, frozen as it pours under the bridge. This is a theme which you will recognize in other Austrian churches, as it was a favorite religious story.

The decoration of the high altar with its double grove of soaring pillars and the *trompe l'oeil* above is especially remarkable. As you leave the church, notice the florid ornamentation of the organ and its gallery.

A turning on the left at the end of the Graben, Kohlmarkt, will lead you directly to Michaelerplatz and the Hofburg.

The Hofburg

The Michaelerplatz, the starting point for visiting the Hofburg is worth exploring on its own account. The Michaelerkirche (St. Michael's Church) takes up one side of the strangely shaped square. It is an amalgam of periods, from Romanesque and Gothic through Baroque and Neo-classical, but the chief effect is Gothic. The interior has some very old frescos and fine carvings. The floor of the nave is indented with tombstones and the high altar seems almost a Baroque afterthought. Near the altar is the tomb of the great 18th-century poet, Pietro Metastasio, who lived in a house on the Michaelerplatz for about 40 years, dying there in 1782. He was court poet in the city during the reign of Maria Theresa, and turned out many opera libretti, at least one of which, *La Clemenza di Tito,* survived changing musical tastes to be set by Mozart.

To the right side of the church, in the Michaeler Passage (go through the arch marked No. 6), is a 16th-century carving of the *Agony in the Garden,* with the Betrayal and Crucifixion shown simultaneously in the medieval manner.

Facing St. Michael's across the square is the flat green facade of the Looshaus (The Loos House). The Griensteidl Café, a famous literary haunt, used to stand here, much frequented by such writers as Schnitzler and the young Hofmannsthal. It was pulled down in 1910 to make way for the present building, the work of Adolf Loos (1870–1933) and the cause of a storm of protest. The windows of Franz Josef's private apartments looked straight out on the new building and, staunch conservative as he was in his tastes, he actually went to law to try and get the "monstrosity" demolished; he called it "the house with no eyebrows". He lost the case. The building was a landmark in undecorated architecture.

Easily eclipsing the Loos House is the great entrance gateway to the Hofburg, the Michaelertor, and the facade on either side, now freshly painted. It is flanked by two well-muscled fountains symbolizing imperial sea and land power. Passing through the triple arch is a main roadway with side walks on each side. Here, under the oval dome, are the entrances into the Imperial Apartments (on the left). These rooms are interesting to visit for the glimpses that they give into the lives and characters of the last Habsburgs, especially of Franz Josef and his wife. Her exercising equipment and other personal effects bear mute witness to the attractive woman who was stabbed by an assassin in Switzerland, after having spent most of her married life wandering the face of Europe in an attempt to avoid the rigid duties that awaited her in Austria.

The Hofburg is like a nest of boxes, courtyards opening off courtyards and wings (trakts) spreading far and wide. A large part of it still houses the offices and conference rooms of the Austrian Government and cannot be visited by the public. This great complex was built at several periods and when each expansion was planned, rather than demolish existing buildings, they were partly adapted and swallowed by the new buildings.

Once through the first, covered courtyard, you are in the In der Burg, with its statue of Franz II. In the left wall is the gateway to the Schweizerhof, the original nucleus of the Hofburg. This gateway is a splendid one, built in 1552, as the inscription at the top says, at the direction of Ferdinand I. It is painted a reddish-brown, black and gold, and gives a fine Renaissance flourish to the facade. The disused moat runs on either hand. Through the Schweizertor lies the Schweizerhof's courtyard with the Hofburgkapelle in one corner. In this Court Chapel, from September to June, high mass is celebrated on Sundays and holidays by the Hofmusikkappelle, made up of the Vienna Boys' Choir, opera singers and musicians from the Vienna Philharmonic Orchestra. Needless to say, it is a musical experience of the first order, so it is essential to buy tickets in advance. They can be obtained on the preceding Friday from 5 P.M. in the Schweizerhof.

The Imperial Treasury

After two years' closure for total renovation, the Imperial Treasury reopened in 1987. Exhibition facilities have been thoroughly modernized to provide a fitting setting for this unique collection.

Among the items of historic significance are a wealth of heraldic objects—tabards, those short tunics that heralds used to wear emblazoned with their masters' coats of arms; staves of office, borne by chamberlains and other officers of the court; huge keys, fit for the castle of a sleeping princess; hoods for falcons; in fact all the panoply of a vast and anciently organized court. The time span covered by the multitude of items, both sacred and secular, is impressive, too. From the Imperial Crown, encrusted with roughly shaped gems and thought to date from about 962, through to objects less than a century old, the collection includes treasures covering some thousand years.

The heart of the Treasury's riches is the Burgundian Treasure, and especially those parts of it connected with the Order of the Golden Fleece. This most romantic of medieval orders of chivalry (which is still in existence) passed into the hands of the Habsburgs when, by marriage, they became Dukes of Burgundy. The Burgundian Treasure encompasses robes, vestments, paintings and jewels and spans several centuries, but of all its evocative pieces the most striking are the church vestments. These form a full set for the celebration of mass; copes, altar cloths, dalmatics and so forth. They are covered with the most delicate and brilliant "needle paintings" of angels, scenes from the bible and saints. These embroideries date from the years before 1477 and rank with such works as the *Très Riches Heures* of the Duc de Berri as masterpieces of medieval creativity.

Here and there in the collection are various objects made of "unicorn" horn—actually narwhal horn. They are touching reminders of that mixture of faith and fantasy that characterized the Middle Ages, for not only was the horn considered a symbol of Christ, but the legend that a unicorn could only be captured by a virgin added to its rarity. One extremely long *ainkhürn,* nearly 8 feet, suggests that the virgin officiating at that particular hunt must have been of quite staggering purity.

Part of the collection's historical relics tells the sad story of the son of Napoleon anad Marie Louise, the King of Rome. Among the more poignant items is the cradle presented by the City of Paris in 1811, no everyday cradle, but more of a cradle-throne from which the baby-king could hold court. It is a happy, elaborate piece of furniture, and not unlike a car from a very aristocratic carousel.

Do not miss the large number of reliquaries, each one containing its fragment of bone, tooth, wood, hair, clothing or other relic of saint or martyr. These reliquaries are often of extremely rich workmanship, encasing their freight of holy detritus in objects of earthly beauty.

And while on the subject of relics, one of the most fascinating is the Holy Lance, supposedly the lance which pierced Jesus' side, into which has been embedded a Holy Nail, wrenched from the Cross. Of great historical interest, too, is a saber, perhaps presented by one legendary hero, Haroun al Raschid, to another, Charlemagne; and a mantle from around 1133, embroidered with two heraldic lions, preying on a couple of prostrate camels, a superb relic of the Norman kings of Sicily.

The Neue Hofburg Museums

Return to In der Burg and turn left, go through the vaulted corridor and out into the openair again. This is the Heldenplatz, the Square of the Heroes. There was a plan, when the Hofburg was being extended in the 1880s, to build two huge sweeping wings, facing each other. Only the wing on the left was actually constructed, the Neue Hofburg. In the center of this great sweep stands the statue of Prince Eugene of Savoy on his rearing steed, while over to your right is the Archduke Karl. The opposite side of the Heldenplatz from where you entered is bounded by the Burgtor, a kind of triumphal arch, dedicated now as a war memorial.

The flight of steps up to the center of the Neue Hofburg will lead you to three museums, the Collection of Weapons, the Ephesus Museum and the Collection of Musical Instruments.

The Epheros (Ephesus) Museum is the newest of the three, and employs the most modern techniques for display. By a clever use of metal scaffolding poles the large sections of masonry rescued during the archeological digs at Ephesus have been placed in exact relation to each other, to give a sense of the scale and form of the original buildings. One of the main features of the exhibition is the remains of a large frieze (dating from the middle of the 2nd century A.D.) from the mausoleum of Lucius Verus, rather in the fashion of latterday Elgin Marbles. It tells of the conquest of the Parthians, confused in movement and without the elegance of its Greek original, but full of vivid details. Also on display are large relief maps, expertly made of wood, which with other models, help the understanding of the terrain that yielded up these fine if fragmented sculptures.

Above the Ephesus Museum is the Collection of Musical Instruments, mentioned at the beginning of this chapter. It is worth visiting, especially if you are interested in early keyboard instruments. On our last visit we had the delight of hearing Beethoven's piano being tuned, and its clear bell-like notes followed us round the galleries like Papageno's magic chimes. The instruments come in all shapes and sizes, a harp in the form of a harpooned fish, a table clavier with drawers and inkwells, one with a curved keyboard, another with the black and white notes reversed. But it is the associations that haunt many of the pianos which make them so interesting. Mahler's piano, one belonging to Brahms, to Clara and Robert Schumann, Haydn's . . . the list is endless. When Mozart called Vienna "Piano Land" he wasn't exaggerating.

The Collection of Weapons (Waffensammlung) is one of the best in the world. The ranks of suits of armor, contained in a maze of rooms, are accompanied by all manner of weapons—swords, crossbows, early guns and pistols, and all backed with fine Flemish tapestry. Many of the pieces are from the most renowned craftsmen of Spain, Italy and Germany. From the Middle Ages up to the 17th century, the possession of the latest fashion in arms and armor was comparable to owning the latest motor car today,

HOFBURG

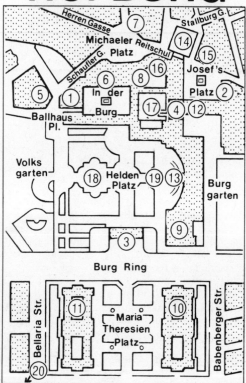

Points of Interest

1 Amelientrakt
2 Augustinerkirche
3 Burgtor
4 Chapel
5 Federal Chancellery
6 Imperial Apartments
7 Michaelerkirche
8 Michaelertrakt
9 Museum of Ethnology
10 Museum of Fine Arts
11 Museum of Natural History
12 National Library
13 Neue Hofburg (entrance to Ephesus, Armor, and Musical Instrument Museums)
14 Palace Stables and Neue Gallerie
15 Pallavicini Palace
16 Riding School
17 Schweizerhof (entrance to Imperial Treasury)
18 Statue of Archduke Karl
19 Statue of Prince Eugene of Savoy
20 Volkstheater

with a similar balance between the utilitarian and the artistic. Here, too, are exotic items captured from the Turks. Not infrequently, as you walk through the rooms, you will see a suit of armor that seems to embody a sense of menace, to have a brooding, threatening life. One can easily understand what a place of terror a medieval battlefield must have been.

There is a fourth museum in the Neue Hofburg, the Museum für Völkerkunde (Ethnographical Museum). The entrance to this one is at the other end of the Neue Hofburg, by the Ring. It is a very rich collection of pieces from all over the world, illuminating societies and cultures not only thousands of miles, but centuries apart. Among the treasures are the robes and head-dress of Montezuma, miracles of feather work. It gives yet another sidelight on the Habsburgs to realize into what remote corners of the world their empire reached.

The Riding School and the New Gallery

If you return to the Michaelerplatz, you can begin to explore the range of buildings that runs to the right, along Augustinerstrasse. The first one, tucked in to the right, is the Winter (or Spanish) Riding School. This is one part of Vienna known throughout the world, for the elegant white Lippizaner horses have become a kind of trademark for the city. For the last 300 years they have been perfecting their *haute école* riding demonstrations, to the sound of Baroque music. The Winter Riding School was built between 1729 and 1735, and once again the architect was Fischer von Erlach.

The breed was started in 1580 and proved themselves in battle as well as in the complicated "dances" for which they are famous today. While it is easy to see them rehearsing, obtaining a ticket for full performances needs planning well in advance.

Across the road from the Riding School (entrance under the colonnade) is the Neue Galerie (New Gallery) in the Stallburg (Palace Stables), which is where the Lippizaners live. You will have to climb two long flights to reach the pictures as there is no elevator. The New Gallery collection is of paintings from the mid-1800s to just after World War I. The rooms are utterly plain, painted white, with the paintings displayed on simple colored screens. The general effect is to show the pictures to the very best advantage. The artists represented range from Millet and Corot, through Delacroix and Courbet (some fine landscapes) to Monet (a luminous garden), Renoir and van Gogh, and end with two fine canvasses by Munch. Along the way there are several German and Austrian contemporaries of these better-known artists, notably Böcklin (with a remarkably pneumatic *Sea Idyll*) and a group by Lovis Corinth, showing his strikingly bold style. There are rarely more than one or two pictures by any single painter, so that the total effect is of an easily assimilable collection of thoroughly representative works. A delight to wander through and highly recommended.

The National Library and the Augustine Church

Return to the colonnade which opens into Josefsplatz, probably Vienna's loveliest square, with a statue of Josef II in the center. The entrance to the National Library, or rather to that part of the National Library that the public most frequently visits, is at the far left corner of the square. As we mentioned before, the Prunksaal (Grand Hall) of the Library is open for only an hour a day in winter (11–12) though from 10–4 in summer, so plan ahead.

This is one of the grandest Baroque libraries in the world, in every sense a cathedral of books. It was created by Fischer von Erlach the younger from the designs of his father, while the frescos in the dome are the work of Daniel Gran and are superb examples of the difficult art of *trompe l'oeil*. The books around the central space under the dome were bought in 1738 from the library of Prince Eugene of Savoy, which contained thousands of priceless items. They are mainly in uniform red bindings. Behind the high ranks of shelves there are hidden bays onto which sections of the shelves open like doors, increasing the shelf capacity tremendously, giving space for scholars to work and preserving the design of the interior. This Library has a higher proportion of manuscripts of textual or artistic importance than any comparable library outside the Vatican.

Opposite the National Library, across Josefsplatz, are the Pallavicini and Palffy Palaces, both built by great families who needed to be near the court. A little further along, at the corner of Augustinerstrasse and Lobkowitz Square, is the Baroque Lobkowitz Palace, built at two periods, with the top floor being by Fischer von Erlach, senior, in 1709. It was here that Beethoven's *Eroica* was first performed. The building has now been lovingly restored and renovated, and houses the Theater Museum.

Turning right out of Josefsplatz you will come to the Augustinerkirche (the Augustine Church) which nestles into the side of the Hofburg as befits a court parish church. It was built soon after 1330 and has a fairly severe interior following heavy restoration in the 1780s. The severity is relieved by two main features, the lovely organ case, painted in gold and white, and the tomb of the Archduchess Maria Christina, the favorite daughter of Maria Theresa. This eye-catching monument is the first thing you see, straight ahead, on entering the church. It is in the form of a white pyramid with mourning figures walking towards an engulfing black doorway. It was by the great Italian sculptor Canova, who first arrived in Vienna in 1797.

In the little crypt of the Chapel of St. George (1337) are the hearts of the Habsburgs in their urns. This is the third place of burial for the scattered remains of the imperial family. But the Augustine Church is not only a place of death, for it was the scene of some famous marriages over the centuries (Napoleon—by proxy—to Marie Louise, and Maria Theresa to Franz of Lothringen), and it is also the place to hear some of the most beautifully performed church music in Vienna. In addition to the magnificent main Rieger organ in the loft, a beautiful Silbermann Bach organ newly built in Holland was installed during 1985 and is also used for concerts.

The Albertina and the Burggarten

The farthest point of this triangular section of the Hofburg contains the Albertina (continue along Augustinerstrasse to the right), called after its founder, Duke Albert of Saxe-Teschen, husband of Maria Christina (she of the Canova tomb). At the risk of sounding over-lyrical, it must be said that the Albertina is one of the greatest collections of graphic art in the world. It contains well over a million items dating back to the 14th century. Not only does it house the founder's own collection, but a multitude of works collected by Prince Eugene together with many later additions.

The fragility of many of the works makes them difficult to display and some are on view in exact replicas. Also, with 50,000 original drawings and 1,200,000 prints, it is impossible to show the whole collection at once, but the Albertina frequently mounts exhibitions of originals which are always worth visiting, and as money permits, conditions are being improved. The most popular part of the collection are the works of Dürer, and especially his *Praying Hands*.

Across the street in the triangular square is the Hrdlicka memorial to victims of World War II, so named for the sculptor who created it and who, in typical Viennese fashion, insisted that if the pieces weren't placed in this spot, he would resign his commission, triggering a dispute which has by no means ended.

Up the steps by the entrance to the Albertina and round the corner of the ramp lies the Burggarten, an attractive small park which contains the only openair statue of the Emperor Franz Josef in Vienna. It stands in a small Japanese-style thicket. There are two other monuments in the Burggarten, one to Mozart, an 1896 conception of the composer, with too many cherubs and an overromanticized statue; the other, large and impressive, to Goethe.

The Academy of Fine Arts and St. Charles's Church

Facing Goethe, across the Opernring, is Schiller. His statue stands in the center of the Schillerplatz, and behind him you will find the Akademie der Bildenden Künste (Academy of Painting and Fine Arts). This art school, founded in 1692, is the oldest art academy in the German-speaking countries. It was declared the "Arts Authority for the Nation" in 1812, and was the responsibility of Metternich from 1818 to 1848. Hitler's antisemitism may have been partly due to his inability to pass the entrance exams, a failure he attributed to the Jewish professors.

While there are many interesting works to see, a *Conversation Piece* by de Hooch, a serene portrait by Rembrandt, eight views of Venice by Francesco Guardi, a Memling *Crucifixion*—the one masterpiece that dwarfs all the others is the *Last Judgement* by Hieronymus Bosch, one of his best works. It is a triptych which tells the story of the Fall of Man, from the beginning in the Garden of Eden on the left-hand panel, to the tortures of Hell on the right-hand one. The Judgement itself and the sins of mankind fill the central section.

From the Academy, Nibelungenstrasse and Friedrichstrasse lead to Karlsplatz, a huge square above the main subway interchange where, outside Josef Olbrich's Sezession, Marc Anthony is seated in a bronze quadriga drawn by four lions. The Sezession, famous but for many years so drab it escaped notice, has just been restored. The "Golden Cabbage" has been regilded, the facade restored to its pristine white, gold and green. Inside, the rooms have been perfectly restored, and in the newly created cellar you can see the restored *Beethoven Frieze* by Gustav Klimt. The attractive cafe will provide a welcome coffee break in stylish surroundings.

Dominating the Karlsplatz is one of Vienna's greatest buildings, the Karlskirche (St. Charles's Church), dedicated to St. Charles Borromeo. It was begun in 1716 by Johann Bernhard Fischer von Erlach and completed after his death by his son, Joseph Emmanuel. The church was, from the first, a slightly disturbing mixture of styles and now with a large reflecting pool in front of it—in which sits a very fine but totally inappropriate

statue by Henry Moore—the effect is of even more artistic confusion, bordering on the bizarre.

The church was another outcome of the plague of 1713, being vowed
by Karl VI, whose name, Charles, was thus linked with Charles Borromeo.
The front of the church is flanked by two great columns, inspired by Trajan's column in Rome. They are out of keeping with the building as a
whole, but were conceived with at least two functions; one was to carry
scenes from the life of the patron saint, carved in imitation of Trajan's
triumphs, and thus help to emphasize the Imperial nature of the building;
and the other was to symbolize the Pillars of Hercules, suggesting the right
of the Habsburgs to their Spanish dominions which the Emperor had been
forced to renounce.

The interior of the church is based on a central oval shape, faced with
chill marble. One is overwhelmingly conscious of a symmetrical and almost musical balance in the way the whole design interacts, leading the
eye always upwards to the great dome, where Rottmayr's superb frescos
open a new heaven. The high altar is illuminated by stiff shafts of gilt sun-
light and cloaked with a penumbra of plaster clouds; not surprisingly it
bears a close affinity to the Plague Column on the Graben. The altar pieces
are by Prokop, Ricci and Gran.

Next to the church is the City Museum, with exhibits showing the history of Vienna. The displays are arranged chronologically and can give the
visitor a very valuable basis of understanding of the way the city developed. Among the items on display are smaller carvings and pieces of
stained glass from the cathedral; flags, banners, portraits and documents,
all imaginatively exhibited. There is also a fair selection of paintings,
Klimt's among them, which have a relevance to the city's history.

Further round the park-like square and above the subway are the two
restored entrances to the city railways by Otto Wagner, once derided, but
now considered attractive examples of Jungendstil.

Beyond the Otto Wagner pavilions is the Musikverein, home of the Vienna Philharmonic. In the glittering Golden Hall and the two smaller
auditoria, some of the best concerts in Vienna are held. Among many other
valuable manuscripts, its library contains original scores by such composers as Beethoven, Brahms, Mozart and Schubert. The Archives may have
some of these treasures on display in the exhibition room upstairs.

Herrengasse and the Scottish Church

From Michaelerplatz, in the opposite direction to Augustinerstrasse,
Herrengasse is lined with interesting buildings, mainly government offices
in former palaces. Number 5 is the early 18th-century Wilczek Palace,
adjoining the Ministry of the Interior which is housed in a 16th-century
palace restored in 1811. Number 9, the 17th-century Mollard-Clary Palace, contains the Museum of Lower Austria, which gives a good idea of
the history of the province as well as of the province's natural history. The
neo-Classical Landhaus, Number 13, seat of the Provincial Government
and Diet of Lower Austria incorporates an early 16th-century chapel by
Anton Pilgram, the sculptor of St. Stephen's.

A left turn (Landhausgasse) leads to the Minoritenplatz, Vienna's quie-
test and most aristocratic square. The 14th-century Minoritenkirche
(Church of the Minor Friars, now Mary of the Snow), damaged during
both Turkish sieges, was restored in the Gothic manner in the late 18th

century. The eight pillars inside divide the nearly square interior into three naves with a floor of plain tiles. There are frescos of heraldic devices on the walls. There is also a large and not entirely successful mosaic copy of Leonardo's *Last Supper* to one side, and a fragment of a fresco of St. Francis.

Among the surrounding palaces, number 1 is the Haus-, Hof- und Staats-archiv (Household, Court and States Archives), whose collection of documents (much of which has now moved to a new building on the outskirts of Vienna), is second only to the Vatican's. Some of this embarrassment of riches is displayed in the fireproof wing of the Bundeskanzleramt (Federal Chancellery), which now also houses the Ministry of Foreign Affairs. It was from this former Court Privy Chancellery, built by Lukas von Hildebrandt on the Ballhausplatz, that the great imperial chancellors determined the fate of Europe. Minoritenplatz 3 is the 17th-century Dietrichstein Palace. Number 5, in the Starhemberg Palace, is the Ministry of Education. It was here that the defender of Vienna against the Turks in 1683 died. Most magnificent is the Liechtenstein Town Palace, which goes through to Bankgasse. This is another palace-lined street and is located between the Burgtheater and the Herrengasse. The Batthyany Palace, the Renaissance Portia Palace and Lukas von Hildebrandt's Kinsky Palace follow one another down it to Freyung, where the Schottenkirche, founded by Duke Jasomirgott in 1155, stands.

The Duke had the Babenberg drive to embellish his court and obviously thought that solid scholarship would help. The monks who gave the foundation its name were actually Irish, not Scottish in the modern use of the word for, in medieval Latin, Ireland was called *Scotia maior*. The church was frequently rebuilt and took its present shape only in the late 1880s. On one side of the various courtyards of the vast Schottenhof, last remodelled in the 1830s, is the Abbey whose Benedictine monks still teach in Austria's oldest High School.

The square beside the church is called Freyung because it commemorates the church's right to grant sanctuary for three days. Opposite the church is the 17th-century Harrach Palace, and, beyond the Austria Fountain whose figures represent the Empire's main rivers, is the vast, imposing Batthyány-Schönborn Palace, a joint enterprise by Fischer von Erlach and Lukas von Hildebrandt (now the Mexican Embassy). Higher up on the Schottengasse—tucked away at the back of a small courtyard on the left— is the Melkstiftkeller, an atmospheric wine cellar.

Between Freyung and Herrengasse is a huge building known as the Palais Ferstl. A beautiful shopping arcade links the two streets and inside they have restored the Cafe Central, once favorite haunt of Lenin, T. Herzl, Karl Kraus and assorted Viennese literary figures, with a lovely staircase. This complex is worth a visit, and if you are lucky, you may even get to see the Grosser Börsesaal, beautifully restored and now a public ballroom and congress hall.

Coming out of the Alte Börse, the second lane on the right is the Naglergasse, leading back to the Graben. What used to be a rather decrepit back street has been newly paved and turned into a chic boutique precinct. A row of five or six medieval houses with early-Baroque frontages have been painstakingly restored to excellent effect.

The Museum of Fine Arts

Across the Burgring from the Heldenplatz and Burgtor is the Maria-Theresien Platz, a formal garden where the focus is a statue of the Empress. It dates from 1880, assembling in one large group below the seated empress, her husband, eldest son, ministers, generals and others who made her reign glorious—Haydn and Mozart among them.

To the left is the Kunsthistorisches Museum (Museum of Fine Arts) and to the right the Naturhistorisches Museum (Museum of Natural History). If natural history interests you, you will be happy to wander in the seemingly endless rooms of stuffed animals on the first floor—but you should be warned that once you get in you may not find it so easy to escape from all those glassy eyes.

The ground floor has prehistoric relics, including many finds from the early Hallstatt civilization. Here, too, is the tiny bulbous *Venus of Willendorf,* some 20,000 years old, carved from limestone and thought to be one of the oldest pieces of sculpture in existence. We warn you, though, you'll have to search for it among much else on display. The Natural History Museum also has collections of meteorites and fossils.

Cross the geometrical gardens to reach the Museum of Fine Arts.

Downstairs are the collections of Egyptian, Greek and Roman art. They are well worth visiting as are the many medieval and Renaissance treasures—including Cellini's glorious gold salt cellar—but space forces us to examine just the painting collection on the first floor.

It is, perhaps, invidious to try to select from the incredible wealth of pictures in the Museum of Fine Arts any for special attention, but, on the other hand, a brief selection might help you to steer around the maze of galleries. The rooms are numbered in two sequences and round two courtyards running clockwise from I–VII (Roman numerals) and 1–13 ordinary numbers; anti-clockwise from IX–XV and 14–24. Room VIII links the two sequences. The rooms with the Roman numerals are the large ones; the smaller, outside rooms, have normal numbering. As you might expect, the large rooms have all the big-scale paintings—some of them striking, some merely pompous; the smaller rooms contain most of the jewel-like pictures, also many of the best portraits. If you suffer from museumitis or are short on time, do the sequences of smaller rooms first. If you have enough time to—take two bites at visiting the Kunsthistorisches Museum, we would heartily advise it. Descriptive information throughout the museum is now in English (and Italian and Japanese) in addition to German.

The museum is undergoing major reconstruction of the upper floors, including the floor that houses its world-famous paintings. Ask for a copy of the free guide leaflet in English at the entry desk; this "floor plan" is a current index to which artists are hung in which rooms. The postcards and reproductions at the sales desk give a clue as to the works the museum (if not the world!) considers the best or most famous in the collection, and if you compare the cards with the artists' names and room numbers on the floor plan, you should be able to find the museum's treasures. The staff is helpful with directions. But this collection is constantly being reshuffled and won't settle down until some future date, when better lighting and air-conditioning installations are completed.

In general, however, the rooms to your right at the top of the stairs will continue to house the works of the Italian, Spanish, and French schools.

Look for the room full of Titians; these give a fine cross-section of portraits and larger compositions. The Tintorettos include his grave signors. The room with the Caravaggios holds his dramatic *David with the Head of Goliath*. The Velazquez portraits of the Habsburgs give a reminder as to how this great collection was indeed formed.

If you move from the Italian, Spanish, and French painters into Room VIII, you begin the transition into the block of rooms at the left of the stairs that house the Dutch and German schools. Here are the hearty Brueghels, which you will instantly recognize, along with Van Dyck, Rubens in both religious and mythical moods, and the great Dúrer portraits of Kleberger and Maximilian I, merciless in their psychological revelation. The peculiar fantasies of Arcimboldo are often out on loan, but the museum seems to have an inexhaustible supply of Rembrandts and Hals to keep the walls covered despite loans to special shows.

The Ring

There are three ways of exploring the Ring. You can ride around it on streetcar 1 or 2; you can walk along it all the way from where it begins by the Danube Canal, at Julius-Raab-Platz, to where it returns to the Canal after its curving flight. Or, and this is the way we recommend, to explore it whenever you happen to cross it on other missions. While it is a pleasant sequence of boulevards, the succession of rather pompous buildings can be a bit overpowering.

There are three points on the Ring we would suggest seeing by themselves. Firstly the Stadtpark, which can be added to your visit to the Karlskirche. It is a romantic park, once dedicated to health cures and now chiefly delightful for visiting an openair café or restaurant, listening to an orchestra playing Viennese music in summer, or looking at the statues of composers, dotted around. The most famous of these is, of course, Johann Strauss himself, fiddling away under the trees and ignoring the symphonic clicking of cameras. Monuments to Bruckner, Franz Lehar, and Robert Stolz are also tucked away here, with Schubert at the other end.

The second stretch of the Ring is that which runs from Maria-Theresien Platz and the great museums along to Rooseveltplatz. This is the part of the Ring that was built up in the secure days of the 1870s and 1880s, where the Parliament Building, the City Hall (Rathaus), the Burgtheater and University all stand, mixtures of Greek revival, Roman and Gothic styles, with a fair measure of Renaissance to hold them together. It makes a pleasant walk, with the Rathauskeller or one of the openair cafés to refresh you *en route*.

At the end of the walk is the Votivkirche, built in 1856–79 to commemorate the escape of the young Franz Josef from the knife of a Hungarian assassin. The Emperor's brother, Maximilian, who died tragically in Mexico, pledged the Votivkirche in thanks. As is often the case with imitative architecture, its mock-Gothic looks tawdry and isn't helped by some truly dreadful modern stained glass and appalling lighting by night.

On this side of town, at Fürstengasse 2, you can find the Palais Liechtenstein (this is the second one, the other is mentioned on page 52), which houses the Museum of Modern Art. The palace was built at the end of the 17th century and is a very large, attractive place, with well-kept grounds and some superb frescos based on the story of Hercules. The collections of modern works assembled in the network of rooms is in strong,

sometimes violent, contrast to their faded elegance. As so often with museums of modern art, where time has not yet had a chance to winnow the
wheat from the chaff, there is a lot of very forgettable stuff on display,
but there are also many pieces that are magnificent. It is well worth while
taking time to explore the maze of rooms, as some of the very best works
are the most deftly hidden. Among the modern masters represented are
Derain, Ernst, Leger, Magritte, Picasso, Lichtenstein, Warhol and many
others.

Across the Danube Canal

On the other side of the Canal from the Inner City you will find two
parks, the Augarten, once Imperial private gardens but opened to the public first in 1775. A part of the main Augarten Palace, built for the widow
of Leopold I, is used by the famous Augarten Porcelain Factory (started
in 1717), and another part as the home of the Vienna Boys' Choir, an integral part of the Hofmusikkapelle.

The other park is the Prater, the leisure grounds of Vienna, with the
wheel (famous from *The Third Man*), a Planetarium, side-shows, some
of the Vienna Fair grounds, a racetrack, golf course and so on. There are
parts, such as Krieau, which are not recommended for idle strolling unless
you happen to be an expert in judo, though these are some way off. A Prater Pass is available to visitors, giving reduced admission to many attrac-
tions.

On the far bank of the Danube, beyond the Prater, is the Donauturm,
the 826-foot tower, with rotating restaurant at 541 feet, and observation
platform at 492 feet. Next to the Donaupark is the Vienna International
Center, a vast complex of highrises round the International Congress Center seating 1,600 in nine halls. Three UN organizations moved in 1979—
the International Atomic Energy Commission, the United Nations Industrial Development Organization and a Palestine refugee section—and their
advent has turned Vienna into the third most important center for the
United Nations. The building costs of 8.5 billion Schilling seem somewhat
disproportionate in comparison with the token rent of 1 Schilling a year,
and it does not have very much to offer to the sightseer. But for those interested, tours are conducted daily, starting at 11 A.M. and 2 P.M., taking about
an hour, from Checkpoint 1. Cost AS40 per person. You will need your
passport or other identification to get into the complex (tel. 2631–4193).

The Belvedere

Where Kärntner and Schubert Ring meet, Schwarzenbergplatz leads
to the Hochstrahlbrunnen, a fountain spurting a jet of water high in the
air, illuminated at night, and the huge Russian War Memorial, whose pro-
letarian realism has been guaranteed by the peace treaty with Russia—
however dearly the Viennese would like to remove it, as it blocks out the
lovely Schwarzenberg Palace, designed by Hildebrandt (outside) and both
Fischer von Erlachs (inside). One wing of the palace is still occupied by
the Schwarzenberg family, the other is a luxury hotel. On the left is the
Rennweg. Number 6 is the entrance to the Lower Belvedere, the country
palace built for Prince Eugene, which consists of two main buildings, one
here at the foot of the hill and the other at the top—the Lower and Upper
Belvedere—with wide formal gardens in between. The whole complex was

masterminded by Hildebrandt and is considered to be one of the most splendid pieces of Baroque architecture anywhere.

The Lower Belvedere contains the Museum of Austrian Baroque, and what better building to house it! This was the home of the prince and the long sequence of lovely rooms now forms the perfect background for the works of art, many of which were created at the time the Belvedere was being built; paintings and sculptures by Daniel Gran, Maulpertsch, Kremser Schmidt, Troger and Georg Raphael Donner. Donner's original lead figures for the Providence Fountain are here. The State Treaty was signed in the Belvedere in 1955 and there is a huge painting of those who took part—it makes an amusing study.

The climb up through the gardens is rewarded by a fine view over Vienna from the terrace, guarded by elegant sphinxes, at the top. The Upper Belvedere was used by the Prince for balls and banquets, and is still used by the Government for such functions. But its main interest lies in the collection of paintings by 19th and 20th century Austrian artists, especially those of Hans Makart, Egon Schiele, Boeckl, Gustav Klimt and Kokoschka. For those who have seen Klimt's work only in reproduction a surprise is in store, for the originals have a richness and incised patterning that gives them an almost three-dimensional quality. These more modern works are on the ground and top floors (with the Klimts and Schieles at the top), while the middle floor contains a lot of mid-19th-century paintings that will, to a non-specialist, seem rather drab. The best scheme is to go right up to the top floor and then work your way down.

The University Botanical Gardens run parallel to the gardens of the Belvedere, while across the Gürtel can be found the Army Historical Museum and the Museum of 20th Century Art. While in the 3rd district, have a cab take you to the corner of Löwengasse and Kegelgasse. There you will see the new apartment house built by the city of Vienna and designed by famous painter Friedensreich Hundertwasser. Not a corner is straight, not a line is horizontal and the facade is filled with trees, golden domes, colored ceramics and countless other details and quotations from other buildings. Hundreds applied for apartments here.

Schönbrunn

Schönbrunn is only a few minutes by subway (U4) from Karlsplatz. You can get off at either the Schönbrunn stop (then walk ahead, or enter the complex from Grünbergstr.) or the Hietzing/Kennedybrücke stop (then walk back). The trip takes a little longer by tram (line 58, from Babenberger Str. and Burgring) up Mariahilferstrasse, main artery leading west, flanked by department stores. You could see the palace and its grounds in a morning, or spend a whole day wandering through the many delights it offers.

It was the favorite residence of the Habsburgs from the time that it was built (1695–1749). Maria Theresa made it her main home, her daughter Marie Antoinette grew up here and carried her memories of Schönbrunn with her to France and to Versailles. Franz Josef was born and died here and preferred to live here above anywhere else. It was also the residence of the last Habsburg Emperor, Karl I, till 1918 and it was here that he abdicated.

The main gates lead into a wide courtyard, the Ehrenhof (Parade Court), bordered by the palace and its wings. To the right is the Coach

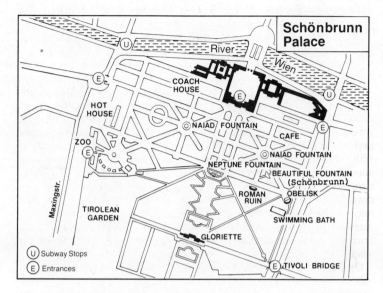

House, Wagenburg, where there is an outstanding collection of ceremonial state coaches, sleighs, hearses, fast private coaches, with the most splendid of all being the Imperial Coronation Coach.

Beside the Coach House is the Rococo Schlosstheater (Palace Theater) now home of a drama school and where performances are given in summer. The theater is beautifully restored, although you will still find a note to the effect that Napoleon witnessed a theatrical performance here.

Of the over 1,440 rooms in the palace, only about 45 can be visited, but those are of great richness and variety.

The tour starts with some of the rooms that Franz Josef and his wife (when she was around) lived in. It is interesting to combine these fairly simple apartments with those in the Hofburg and come up with a fairly clear picture of the kind of life that the old autocrat lived. You will see here the simple iron bedstead on which he died on November 21, 1916. Memories of Maria Theresa and Marie Antoinette come next and are followed by the prettiest sequence of rooms, starting with the Blue Chinese Drawingroom, rich with "Indian" wallpaper and eastern furnishings. The Vieux-Laque Room was a favorite with Maria Theresa, interesting for its Viennese Rococo and black lacquer panels and Chinoiserie decorations, the colored wood flooring is especially noteworthy. Then come the Napoleonic echoes, his own bedroom followed by more Maria Theresa chambers—the Porcelain Room, with around 210 blue ink drawings; the "Millions" Rooms, paneled in a special rosewood, framing in gilt 260 Indian miniatures done on vellum; the Tapestry Room, with its view of Crown Prince Rudolf's private garden. In the Duke of Reichstadt Room the Napoleonic echoes come back in full force, for this is where his son died at the age of 21 of tuberculosis.

The procession of smaller rooms is interrupted halfway round by the great state rooms—especially the Great Gallery, which has featured in many films and is the central glory of Schönbrunn's interior. The ceilings are magnificently frescoed, and one of the sections—that on the east end of incidents in the Seven Years' War—is a modern version, replacing the 18th-century one destroyed in a 1945 air raid.

The Chapel, which you can visit on the way out of the State Apartments, is fairly restrained, when compared with the riot of decorative excess upstairs, but it still houses one or two quiet masterpieces. It dates from 1700, and was slightly altered in Maria Theresa's reign.

Behind the palace lies the large formal park, divided by 40-foot hedges whose geometrically exact tops seem to have been clipped by a pair of celestial shears. The park contains several lovely fountains—two of which are especially attractive; the Schöner Brunnen (Beautiful Fountain), which gave the palace its name, and the Neptune Fountain, dating from 1780 with its triumphant statuary (it only plays in summer). Near to the Schöner Brunn you will find the Roman Ruins, a fake collection of ancient elements, grouped around a reedy pond. It is often besieged by art students, trying to out-draw Piranesi. Another point to head for is the Obelisk, with its fountain, pool and grotto. This 1777 theatrical fantasy terminates a striking view. Also in the gardens is one of the oldest zoos in Europe (founded in 1752) and probably the only Baroque-style zoo anywhere.

On the rising ground at the other side of the park is the colonnaded hall, the Gloriette, surmounted by an Imperial Eagle. It was originally hoped to build the palace on this eminence, but it proved to be impractical. From here, by climbing the winding staircase at one end, there is an extraordinary view across Schönbrunn and its grounds to the city and the Vienna Woods beyond.

Close to the Meidling Gate there is a pleasant outdoor cafe tucked under the trees. It makes an ideal spot for lunch on a summer visit.

PRACTICAL INFORMATION FOR VIENNA

ARRIVING IN VIENNA. By Plane. You can change your money and reserve your hotel room at the airport, if you need to. The airport bus takes you downtown to the City Air Terminal behind the Stadtpark, beside the Hilton Hotel, in about 30 minutes; the buses leave every 20 minutes. Fare—75 sch. Be sure you get the right bus; buses also go to the Westbahnhof via the Südbahnhof. There is now direct fast-train (S-Bahn) service from the airport (underground) to the Terminal at the Hilton. Trains run roughly every hour. A taxi into town from the airport costs about AS350.

By Train. You will end up at either *Westbahnhof* (West Station) if coming from Germany, Switzerland or western parts of Austria, or at *Südbahnhof* (South Station) if coming from southern parts of Austria or Italy. In each there is a Room Information Office *(Information-Zimmernachweis)*. Both will make room reservations as well as provide other information.

By Boat. Praterlände/Reichsbrücke, on the main course of the Danube, is only a short taxi ride from the U Bahn station on the Vorgartenstrasse; slightly longer to the city center (taxis wait at the arrival of the ship). During summer information can be obtained from Vienna Tourist Association hostesses on incoming ships and at the landing stage.

TOURIST INFORMATION. For general holiday information on all of Austria inquire at the offices of the *Fremdenverkehrswerbung,* the Austrian National Tourist Office, Margaretenstr. 1, 1040 (587 20 00). Current events (theater performances, concerts, etc.) are given in German and English by telephone (dial 15 15) on a 24-hour basis.

City Tourist Information. *Fremdenverkehrsstelle der Stadt Wien,* Vienna City Tourist Office, with office in the Kärntner Strasse 38, tel. 513 88 92, open daily 9–7 for information on the city of Vienna but not room reservation.

For room reservation you may apply to the following offices:

Information-Zimmernachweis at Westbahnhof, West Station (83 51 85), open daily from 6.15 A.M. to 11 P.M.

Information-Zimmernachweis at Südbahnhof, South Station (65 21 68), open daily from 6.15 A.M. to 10 P.M.

Vienna Booking Service, Opernpassage (586 23 46), open Mon.–Sat. 9–6, Sun. 9–2.

Tourist information and room reservation office at the airport, open from 9 A.M. to 10.30 P.M. (7770–2617).

Tourist Information at Novotel on Westautobahn all year; Rasthaus Föhrenberg on Südautobahn, from April to end of Oct.; 9 A.M. to 7 P.M. both; *Information-Zimmernachweis* at the end of the Westautobahn (97 12 71); *Information-Zimmernachweis* at the end of the Südautobahn, Triesterstr. 149 (67 41 51). Information point at DDSG docking station on the Danube, Handelskai. (218 01 14).

Guides. Inquire in writing to *Verein der Geprüften Fremdenführer,* A-1130 Vienna, Montecuccolipl. 1–3. Vienna Guide Service member Charlotte Speiser, A-1220 Vienna, Rennbahnweg 27 (51 45 00) can help; or contact *Sektion Fremdenverkehr* (Tourist Section) (tel. 514 50 0) at the Chamber of Commerce. Also *Fremdenführerzentrale,* A-1090, Boltzmanngasse 19 (31 42 43). A half day on foot or by car will cost AS800. Also check the Vienna Guide Service branch at tel. 74 52 02. A 1½-hour guided group tour will cost about AS95 per person.

Embassies and Consulates. *British Embassy and Counsulate,* A-1030, Jauresgasse 10 (755 61 17); *Canadian Embassy,* A-1010, Dr. Karl Luegerring 10 (533 36 91). *U.S. Consulate,* A-1010 Gartenbaupromenade 2 (51451).

Motoring Information. *Österreichischer Automobil-, Motorrad- und Touring Club* (ÖAMTC), Schubertring 1–3 (711 99 70) and on the main road in from the airport at Schwechat (777277), open daily (including holidays) until 8 P.M., for emergency repairs also (95 40). Nationwide emergency repair (120). Traffic and road information (1590).

Lost and Found. Fundamt (Police), 1090 Vienna, Wasagasse 22 (31 66 110); Fundamt (Railways), Westbahnhof (56 50–29 96).

Escort Service and Baby Sitters. For these services, as well as for interpreters, translators or help in driving, contact the Meeting Center of the *Österreichischer Akademischer Gästedienst* (Austrian Student Society Service), Mühlgasse 20, 1040 (587 35 25). They have 2,400 students (male and female) on their rolls who are willing to help you.

Emergencies. If you need a doctor and don't speak any German, try *American Medical Society of Vienna,* Lazarettgasse 13 (42 45 68), or call your embassy. In case of an accident, call 133 for Police Accident Squad, and 144 for ambulance service.

Youth Hostels. *Verein der Wiener Jugendherbergen,* 1200, Friedrich-Engels-Platz 24 (35 07 51).

English Language Radio. "Blue Danube Radio" FM102.5, news, music and information in English from 7–9 A.M., 12–2 P.M. and 6–8 P.M. in Vienna area only. The 12–2 programming block is also carried nationwide on the sound channel of the second television program (FS2).

VIENNA DISTRICTS. Vienna is divided into 23 districts, and, if you are to get to know the city, it is as well to have some idea of how the system works and where the districts fall. The districts are numbered by a postal code which is based on the figure of 1000; the center two digits are changed—thus the 1st District (Inner City) is 1010, and the other end of the scale, the 23rd District, is 1230.

Area Code. The area code for phoning Vienna from outside is 0222.

HOTELS. Unless you are motorized—and particularly if you have only a short time to spend in Vienna—you will want to stay in the Inner City (1010), within walking distances of the most important sights, restaurants and shops. Besides, the best way to see Vienna is by strolling around, and this is done more easily if your base is not too far away.

The Inner City has all kinds of hotels, but mostly in the upper grades. There is a fair grouping of moderate and inexpensive ones in the Mariahilferstrasse-Westbahnhof (West Station) area, also within easy reach of most of the Inner City. The hotels a little further out can easily be reached by a short streetcar ride, or even on the subway if you are lucky.

If you are ready to take public transport, it can be a good idea to stay in the green districts, in some small hotel in the Schönbrunn area or outside of the Gürtel (Beltway).

From Easter through October it is advisable to make reservations in advance, as the tourist season is extended at each end by large international conventions. During the Vienna Fair in September, you might have to move further afield to nearby towns such as Tulln (try *Zur Rossmühle*) or Deutsch Wagram *(Marchfelderhof)* with hourly commuter trains to Vienna.

Following is our selection from several hundred hotels available. Within each grade all listings are alphabetical and represent no particular order of preference. All rooms with baths or showers unless otherwise stated; color television usually in the two top categories.

The City Tourist Office has several bureaux to help with accommodations if you are in any difficulty, see *Tourist Information* above.

Luxury

Ambassador, 1010, Neuer Markt 5 (51 4 66). On the square with the famous Donner Fountain, flanked on the other side by Kärntnerstrasse, the world-famous, elegant shopping street in the heart of Vienna. A favorite of diplomats, it has a long tradition of catering to important personalities, including Theodore Roosevelt and Mark Twain. The red brocade walls in the suites and the public rooms, including the restaurants, glitter from chandeliers. 106 airconditioned rooms at the lower price range in this category. AE, DC, MC, V.

Bristol, 1010, Kärntnerring 1 (51516–536). Along from the Opera, one of the venerable Vienna hotels. Founded in 1894, it has preserved its inimitable personality—a fine blend of tradition, elegance and Viennese *savoir-*

faire. 152 rooms, several plush suites; excellent *Korso* restaurant and pleasantly comfortable bar. Special executive club floor. AE, DC, MC, V.

De France, 1010, Schottenring 3 (34 35 40). Near Votivkirche. 230 rooms (those on the courtside are quieter). Restaurant and bar. AE, DC, MC, V.

Hilton, 1030, Am Stadtpark (75 26 52). Above the City Air Terminal, just beyond the Ring. 620 airconditioned rooms and 8 penthouse suites; one of the more attractive of this chain. Fine food in *Prinz Eugen* restaurant, one of the best in the city and much frequented by the Viennese themselves. *Vindobona* wine cellar; bar, cafe, health club with sauna, garage. Executive facilities. AE, DC, MC, V.

Imperial, 1010, Kärntnerring 16 (50 1 10–0). Near the Opera. This almost 100-year-old palace of imperial fame and elegant appearance is the top hotel in the city. Old traditions and modern comfort are reflected in antique furnishings and up-to-date facilities. A large painting of the old Emperor Franz Josef presides over the palatial stairway. Visiting heads of state and other leading dignitaries stay here. All 160 rooms are spacious and have baths with heated floors. Distinguished restaurant *Zur Majestat,* and cafe with Viennese music; cozy and intimate bar. AE, DC, MC, V.

Marriott, 1010, Parkring (51 5 18). Across from the Stadtpark, and an easy stroll to the city center. 304 luxury rooms, sauna, fitness room, indoor pool, good restaurants, particularly for Sunday brunch. 400-car garage. AE, DC, MC, V.

Palais Schwarzenberg, 1030, Schwarzenbergplatz 9 (78 45 15). A small and exclusive hotel in a wing of the Baroque palace still owned by Prince Schwarzenberg; 42 beds, all rooms with authentic period furnishings, most overlooking the garden. Uniquely quiet location off the very center of the city. Large parking area in the palace courtyard. Excellent restaurant and bar, with glorious terrace in garden. AE, DC, MC, V.

Plaza, 1010, Am Schottenring 1 (31390). Vienna's newest luxury hotel, associated with the Hilton chain. 252 rooms, all imaginable facilities, including sauna, fitness room, garage, restaurants. AE, DC, MC, V.

Sacher, 1010, Philharmonikerstr. 4 (51 4 56). Behind the Opera; legendary; original oil paintings, sculptures and *objets d'art* decorate the halls and rooms. Other treasures of the old days include a tablecloth embroidered with signatures of most of the famous crowned and "decrowned" heads of state of seven decades. A portrait of the redoubtable Frau Sacher looks over the bar; her husband Eduard Sacher, a famous chef, left as his legacy the recipe for *Sachertorte,* the world famous chocolate cake. See also *Restaurants.* AE, DC, MC.

SAS Palais, 1010, Parkring (51 5 17–0). Old Ringstrasse Palais rebuilt to house luxury hotel. 165 rooms, bar, restaurant. Ideal for businessmen who like to be housed in style. AE, DC, MC, V.

Vienna Intercontinental, 1030, Johannesgasse 28 (71122). Overlooking the City Park. 500 rooms, streamlined modern comfort; extensive convention facilities. Excellent *Four Seasons* gourmet restaurant; pleasant Brasserie. 250-car underground garage. AE, DC, MC, V.

Expensive

Amadeus, 1010, Wildpretmarkt 5 (63 87 38). Near St. Stephen's. 30 rooms, with mini-bar. Breakfast only. AE, DC.

Am Parkring, 1010, Parkring 12 (512 65 24). 65 airconditioned rooms on 11th and 13th floors, overlooking the City Park, garage. AE, DC, MC, V.

Alba Palace, 1050, Margaretenstr. 92 (55 46 86). 117 comfortable rooms, restaurant, garage. AE, MC, DC, V.

Ananas, 1050, Rechte Wienzeile 101 (55 56 21). Famous *art nouveau* printing works turned into a top-rate hotel. 536 rooms in different categories. 3 restaurants, bars, cafes. AE, DC, MC, V.

Astoria, 1010, Kärntnerstr. 32 (51 57 70). Entrance from Führichgasse. Old and traditional; 108 modernized rooms and good restaurant. AE, DC, MC, V.

Biedermeier, 1030, Landstrasse Hauptstr. 28 (75 55 75). 204 rooms with every comfort in a beautifully renovated 1820s house. Cafe, heuriger, restaurant. A genuine touch of old Vienna. AE, DC, MC, V.

Europa, 1010, Neuer Markt 3 (51 5 94). In the heart of the city. The best of its 102 airconditioned rooms are in the corners of the building. Evening musical entertainment in the restaurant, and a really dry martini in the little bar upstairs; large cafe on the ground floor. AE, DC, MC, V.

Graben, 1010, Dorotheergasse 3 (512 15 31). Just off Graben. 46 rooms, most with bath, rest with shower. Restaurant with diet specialties. AE, DC, MC, V.

Josefshof, 1080, Josefsgasse 4 (43 89 01–0). 38 rooms in Biedermeier style. A hotel to live in. Spacious rooms most with kitchen area. Sauna, buffet breakfast; quiet with garage. AE, DC, MC, V.

K & K Palais Hotel, 1010, Rudolfsplatz 11 (533 13 530). 66 rooms with every comfort. Modern and airy. AE, DC, MC, V.

Kaiserin Elisabeth, 1010, Weihburggasse (51 5 26–0). Near St. Stephen's; old, with 73 rooms, most with bath, some with shower. Homey atmosphere, good value. Once housed Wagner and Liszt. AE, DC, MC, V.

König von Ungarn, 1010, Schulerstr. 10 (515 84). Just behind St. Stephen's. 32 rooms, newly-restored but maintaining old traditions with a fine sense of style. Attractive indoor courtyard bar. Restaurant is in the next door house where Mozart once lived. AE, DC, MC, V.

Kummer, 1060, Maria Hilferstr. 71a (58895). 110 rooms, all with bath or shower. DC, MC, V.

Mailbergerhof, 1010, Annagasse 7 (512 06 41–0). In the center. 40 rooms. Breakfast only. An old house with lovely arcaded courtyard. AE, DC, V.

Mercure, 1010, Fleischmarkt la (53460). New hotel in good location. 105 rooms with every comfort. Seminar facilities. Restaurant. AE, DC, MC, V.

Opernring, 1010, Opernring 11 (587 55 18–0). Across from the Opera; 35 rooms, breakfast only. Inside rooms are quieter but lack the magnificent view of the Ring and Opera House. Unusually pleasant, personal touch. AE, DC, MC, V.

Prinz Eugen, 1040, Wiedner Gürtel 14 (505 71 41). Opposite South Station and near Belvedere Palace. 106 rooms, some with terrace and fine views, but noisy on the street side. Restaurant. AE, DC, MC, V.

Rathauspark, 1010, Rathausstr, 17 (42 36 61). Old building completely modernized. 117 rooms, comfortable and convenient. AE, DC, MC, V.

Römischer Kaiser, 1010, Annagasse 16 (512 77 51). Romantik Hotel. Central; 27 rooms in a Baroque palace; bar, breakfast only. AE, DC, MC, V.

Royal, 1010, Singerstr. 3 (512 46 31). Near Graben and St. Stephen's. 81 spacious rooms, on the top floor with terrace; some elegant suites. Bar and Italian restaurant, *Firenze.* AE, DC, MC, V.

Scandic Crown, 1020, Handelskai 269 (217 77). Impressive former warehouse directly on the Danube now turned into vast, luxurious hotel. 367 rooms. Restaurants, tennis courts and countless other facilities. 30 mins to city center via streetcar and subway. AE, DC, V.

Tourotel, 1100, Kurbadstr. 8 (68 16 31). 256 rooms; indoor pool, solarium, fitness room and sauna; garage, bar and restaurant. 45 mins from city center by direct streetcar line 67. AE, DC, MC, V.

Moderate

Albatros, 1090, Liechtensteinstr. 89 (34 35 08). Near U.S. Embassy. 70 airconditioned rooms; sauna, indoor pool, solarium; garage; bar and restaurant. AE, DC, MC, V.

Am Stephansplatz, 1010, Stephansplatz 9 (534 050). Across from St. Stephen's Cathedral. 66 rooms, most with bath or shower; those at the front offer magnificent views of the cathedral. Cafe. AE, DC, V.

Austria, 1010, Wolfengasse 3 (51 5 23). Near the main Post Office. 51 rooms, most with bath or shower. In quiet side street. AE, DC, MC, V.

Erzherzog Rainer, 1040, Wiedner Haupstr. 27–29 (501 110). Near Karlsplatz. 85 rooms, most with bath; those on streetside can be noisy. Fine restaurant. AE, DC, MC, V.

Fürstenhof, 1070, Neubaugürtel 4 (93 32 67). Close to Westbahnhof. Excellent value, spacious, old-fashioned comfort. Cool in summer. All rooms with shower. AE, DC, MD, V.

Ibis, 1060, Mariahilfergürtel 22–4 (56 56 26). 350 rooms, modern, convenient for Westbahnhof; efficient. Surprisingly good restaurant.

Kärntnerhof, 1010, Grashofgasse 4 (512 19 23). Near main Post Office. 45 rooms, all with bath or shower. Good breakfast, friendly. AE, DC, MC, V.

Savoy, 1070, Lindengasse 12 (93 46 46). Modern. 43 rooms; garage. AE, DC, MC, V.

Stefanie, 1020, Taborstr. 12 (21 15 0). Across the Danube canal. 130 rooms, all with bath. Garage, bar, and restaurant. AE, DC, MC, V.

Westbahn, 1150, Pelzgasse 1 (92 14 80). 63 rooms, some with bath or shower. Bar, garage. AE, DC, MC, V.

Westminster, 1090, Harmoniegasse 5 (34 66 04). Near U.S. Embassy. 75 rooms, most with bath. Garage, bar. AE, DC, MC, V.

Wilhelminenberg, 1160. Savoyenstr. 2 (78 66 26). Neo-empire Schloss on the edge of the Vienna Woods overlooking city, built for Archduke Rainer and now converted into a hotel. 96 rooms with shower. About an hour by streetcar and bus from city center. Very comfortable and excellent value. Terrace cafe.

Wimberger, 1070, Neubaugürtel 34 (93 76 36). 97 rooms, some with bath or shower. Well known restaurant and café. MC, V.

Inexpensive

Carlton-Opera, 1040, Schikanedergasse 4 (56 42 15). In quiet side street. 53 rooms, some with shower. Bar and restaurant. AE, DC, MC, V.

Europhaus Wien, 1140, Linzer Str. 429 (97 25 36). Rosenhotel. 22 rooms with bath. Garden. 45 mins from city center by bus and subway or streetcar.

Gabriel, 1030, Landstrasser Hauptstr. 165 (72 67 54). 29 rooms, most with bath or shower, parking. AE, MC.

Gloriette, 1140, Linzer Str. 105 (92 35 33). Not far from Schönbrunn; ask for a quiet room. 60 rooms, 12 with shower. Parking, restaurant.

Goldenes Einhorn, 1050, Am Hundsturm 5 (55 47 55). 17 rooms, some with bath or shower. Old type of family-run *Gasthaus.*

Goldene Spinne, 1030, Linke Bahngasse la (72 44 86). Near City Air Terminal. 43 rooms, some with bath or shower. Bar and restaurant.

Kugel, 1070, Siebensterngasse 43 (93 33 55). Near the Messepalast. 37 rooms, 3 baths, 24 showers.

Mariahilf, 1060, Mariahilferstr, 121B (597 36 05). 75 rooms, some with bath or shower. AE, DC, MC, V.

Post, 1010, Fleischmarkt 24 (51 58 30). Opposite the main Post Office. 106 rooms, some with bath or shower. AE, DC, MC, V.

Rathaus, 1080, Langegasse 13 (43 43 02). 37 rooms with shower.

Rosenhotel International, 1080, Buchfeldg. 8 (43 52 91). 54 rooms with shower. Garage, bar. AE, MC, V.

Schweizerhof, 1010, Bauernmarkt 22 (533 19 31). Central. 55 rooms, 48 showers, 7 baths. Restaurant. AE.

Strudlhof, 1090, Pasteurgasse 1 (31 25 22). Near U.S. Embassy. 48 rooms, all with bath. Garage, bar, and restaurant. AE, DC, MC, V.

Wandl, 1010 Petersplatz 9 (53 45 50). near Graben. 137 rooms, some with bath or shower. Facing the Barquoe St. Peter's Church. Bar.

Zur Wiener Staatsoper, 1010, Krugerstr. 11 (513 12 74). 22 rooms, conveniently situated. AE.

Pensions

There are quite a few pensions in Vienna but their rates are only slightly lower than the corresponding hotel categories. Those classified as top category are sometimes overpriced for the type of accommodations offered. The service personnel may be of lower quality, too. Simply getting into pensions can be a problem—they are often located on the top floors of large buildings, the lifts can be out of order, stairway lights switch off automatically—usually when you are catching your breath between floors—and, to round it off, the building doorman may well be out so you have to remember to carry a key. It sounds like home from home!

The pensions in outlying districts, however, are usually located in separate buildings of their own and are more like normal hotels than the old-fashioned Inner City brand of pension.

Expensive

Arenberg, 1010, Stubenring 2 (512 19 11). 25 rooms, all with bath or shower. In Inner City. Parking. AE, MC, V.

Barich, 1030, Barichgasse 3 (712 12 73). 17 rooms, all but one with bath or shower. Bar, garage.

Domizil, 1010, Schulerstr. 14 (513 30 93). 44 beds, newly opened, every comfort, although at the highest price of any pension. Buffet breakfast. Central; ask for second floor rooms at back. AE, DC, MC, V.

Rothensteiner Appartements, 1070, Neustiftgasse 66 (93 96 43). 19 rooms, all with bath. Parking. Atmospheric cellar-restaurant with good wine and Austro-Greek specialties. Open late.

Sacher Appartements, 1010, Rotenturmstr. 1 (533 32 38). No relation of the hotel of same name. Next to St. Stephen's cathedral. Tops in this category; spacious and friendly.

Wiener, 1010, Seilergasse 16 (512 48 16). 11 rooms, all with bath. Bar. At the top of this category.

Moderate

Some of the best of this category are in the suburban districts.

Christina, 1010, Hafnersteig 7 (533 29 61). 33 rooms, all with bath or shower. In the Inner City. Bar. MC.

City, 1010, Bauernmarkt 10 (63 95 21). 12 rooms, all with bath or shower. In the Inner City; restaurant. AE, DC.

Geissler, 1010, Postgasse 14 (533 28 03). 22 rooms, 3 with bath, 13 with shower. Garage and restaurant. Inner City. AE, DC, MC, V.

Kurpension Oberlaa, 1100, Kurbadstr. 6 (68 36 11). 40 rooms, all with shower. Sauna, indoor pool, solarium, fitness room and cure facilities; restaurant and parking. 45 mins by direct streetcar to city center. AE, DC.

Museum, 1070, Museumstr. 3 (93 44 26). 15 rooms, all with bath or shower. Garage, restaurant. AE, MC.

Neuer Markt, 1010, Seilergasse 9 (512 23 16). Inner City. 37 rooms, most with bath or shower. Restaurant for guests only. AE, DC, MC, V.

Nossek, 1010, Graben 17 (533 70 41). 26 rooms, some with bath or shower. Restaurant. Inner City. Reader recommended.

Inexpensive

Astra, 1090, Alser Str. 32 (42 43 54). 24 rooms, most with shower. AE.

Auer, 1090, Lazarettgasse 3 (43 21 21). Near the General Hospital. 14 rooms, only 2 with shower. DC, MC, V.

Austria, 1090, Garnisongasse 7 (42 21 36). Near Votivkirche. 13 rooms, some with bath or shower.

Felicitas, 1080, Josefsgasse 7 (42 72 12). Clean and friendly. Some rooms with shower.

Milanohof, 1170, Neuwaldegger Str. 44 (46 14 97). 11 rooms, all with showers. Restaurant, diet specialties.

Zipser, 1080, Langegasse 49 (42 02 28). Good value. All rooms with shower. V.

Seasonal Hotels

An excellent bargain are the student homes which operate as seasonal hotels between July and September. Single or double rooms, all with baths or showers. All Rosenhotels can be booked by calling 59 70 68–0.

Moderate

Academia, 1080, Pfeilgasse 3a (43 16 61). 368 rooms; the most luxurious, TV, bar and restaurant. AE, MC, V.

Avis, 1080, Pfeilgasse 4–6 (42 63 74–0). 72 rooms; bar and restaurant. AE, MC, V.

Panorama, 1200, Brigittenauer Lände 224–228 (35 15 41). A little far out, thus the cheapest for the usual fitness rooms, sauna, TV. 356 rooms, bar and restaurant. Parking.

Rosen-hotel Burgenland 1, 1090, Wilhelm-Exner-Gasse 4 (43 91 22). 71 rooms; suana, pool and fitness room; bar and restaurant. AE, MC, V.

Rosen-hotel Burgenland 2, 1060, Mittelgasse 18 (596 12 47–0). 150 rooms; sauna, fitness room; garage, bar and restaurant. AE, MC, V.

Rosen-hotel Burgenland 3, 1060, Burgerspitalg 17 (597 94 75–0).

Rosen-hotel Niederosterreich, 1020, Untere Augartenstr. 31 (35 35 26). 100 rooms; sauna, fitness room; garage, bar and restaurant. AE, MC, V.

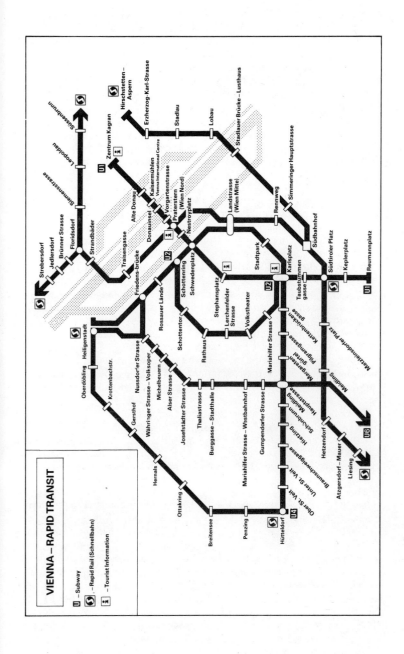

VIENNA – RAPID TRANSIT

Ⓤ – Subway

Ⓢ – Rapid Rail (Schnellbahn)

ℹ – Tourist Information

Inexpensive

Alsergrund, 1080, Alser Str. 33 (43 32 31). 58 rooms, TV and restaurant.
Auersperg, 1080, Alser Str. 9 (43 25 49). 80 rooms. MC.
Haus Döbling, 1190, Gymnasiumstr. 85 (34 76 31). 550 rooms. Restaurant with diet cooking. Parking.
Haus Dr. Schärf, 1200, Lorenz-Müller-Gasse 1 (33 81 71). 130 rooms, TV, bar, restaurant and parking.
Josefstadt, 1080, Buchfeldgasse 16 (43 52 11). 40 rooms. TV and restaurant. MC, V.

GETTING AROUND VIENNA. By Subway. Travelers with one eye on the budget would find it advisable to get acquainted with Vienna's public transport system. There are streetcars (trams), buses, a subway, and there is also a *Schnellbahn* (fast railway) serving primarily the northeast, northwest, and southeast suburbs, including the airport.

Of the *U-Bahn* (subway), the U1 runs from Reumannplatz in the 10th District via Stephansplatz, Praterstern, to the Vienna International Center and Zentrum Kagran on the other side of the Danube. The U2 rings the Inner City from Schottenring to Karlsplatz. And the U4 covers Heiligenstadt (Vienna 19), Schwedenplatz (Danube Canal), Karlsplatz, Schönnbrunn and Hütteldorf. You will find the U-Bahn easy to use, with clear colored plans to facilitate travel. The U6 line links Heiligenstadt or Friedensbrücke (be sure to check the destination signs!) and runs along the Gürtel, including a stop at the Westbahnhof, before heading south to Meidling and on to Siebenhirten.

By Streetcar and Bus. In most busy areas, such as would be frequented by a tourist, the streetcars tread on one another's heels. They start at an incredibly early hour of the morning and continue, usually to between 11 and 12 at night. At each streetcar stop there is a sign which tells what cars stop there, where these cars are going and at what hours the first and last trips of the day are made.

Special city buses operate in the Inner City weekdays 7 A.M.–8 P.M. and Sat. until 2 P.M. Numbers 1A, 2A, 3A. At weekends night buses marked "N" operate at half-hourly intervals in all directions from Schwedenplatz. Cost AS25.

If you can't figure out the system yourself, your hotel porter or desk clerk can steer you to the right stop and tell you how to proceed.

There are public transport information booths in the Karlsplatz underpass (587 31 86), open Mon.–Fri. 7–6, Sat. and Sun. 8.30–4, and in the Stephansplatz underpass (52 42 27), open Mon.–Fri. 8–6, Sat. and Sun. and holidays 8.30–4.

Tickets for buses, streetcars and Stadtbahn cost AS20 if bought singly; AS14 if bought in advance in strips of 4 at a *Tabak Trafik* (tobacco store). With a single ticket, cars and means of transport can be changed if continuing in same direction without breaking the journey. Most streetcars have automatic ticket machines in the first car (marked by a yellow sign). They swallow 5 and 10 schilling coins, so have them handy. A 3-day network ticket costs AS102. An 8-day ticket is available for AS 220. This can be used on 8 separate days or by up to 8 people on one day.

Taxis in Vienna charge according to the meter, and they are comparatively cheap; luggage costs AS 10 per case. A tip of 10% is the usual. Taxis can be taken at the stands, which are numerous in the Inner City, or ask a hotel doorman to help. For radio-directed taxis dial 31 30, 601 60, or 43 69.

Horse Cabs. You can still get a *Fiaker,* the Vienna horsecab, on Helden-platz, Stephansplatz and in front of Albertina, or even order one for a longer ride or a special occasion. Enjoyable but expensive. For longer trips check the price in advance.

By Car. The speed limit within the city limits is 50 km. (about 31 miles) per hour. Honking is forbidden unless absolutely necessary. Priority at intersections not otherwise marked is always to the car on the right. Street-cars (trams) have the right-of-way even when approaching from the left.

Parking. During the daytime it is quite difficult to find parking space in the inner city. In many streets in the center permitted parking time is limited to 1½ hours. In some of these areas special parking tickets are required, available at a Tabak Trafik (tobacco shop) or bank—they come in 3 colors: red for ½ hour, blue for 1 hour, green for 1½ hours, and cost AS 5 per 30 minutes. Parking is forbidden from December–May on all streets with streetcar tracks. There are several large underground parking garages, including Am Hof square near Graben, Karlsplatz, on Kärntner-str., beside the Opera (there is an underground connection between the garage and the Opera), behind the Cathedral, Franz Josefs Kai near the Rotenturmstr., and on the Ring in front of the Rathaus. The last two tend to be less full. Many shops give a free hour's parking in one of these for every AS 300 spent.

Road Information. Call up 15 90 for recorded and information messages provided by the Austrian Automobile Club.

Car Hire. A variety of self-drive cars can be rented from *Budget Renta-car,* Hotel Hilton, (75 65 65), and at airport (7770–2711); *Carop,* Mollard-gasse 15 (597 16 75), and at airport (7770–2699); *Denzel,* 1010, Kärntner-ring 14 (65 44 81) and at airport (7770–3316); *Hertz,* Kärntnerring 17 (512 86 77); *Avis,* Opernring 1 (587 35 95); and at airport (7770–2700); *Inter-Rent Austria,* Schubertring 7 (75 67 17), and at airport (7770–2990), most-ly VWs, will deliver the car to your hotel. A number of firms provide you with chauffeur-driven cars ranging from Cadillac to Volkswagen bus and with drivers who speak several languages; among them: *Goth,* 1030, Jo-hannesg. 28 (in Hotel Intercont.) (713 71 96); *Franz Mazur,* Hasengasse 18 (604 22 33); *Kalal,* 1030, Rennweg 73 (715 59 25); also in Graz, Linz, Salzburg. *Buchbinder,* 1034, Schlachthausgasse 38 (712 26 43) rents cars at particularly favorable rates.

SEASONAL EVENTS. A monthly guide of events is available at all information centers without charge. The outstanding event of the winter season is Fasching, carnival season, which lasts from New Year's Eve until Mardi Gras. Hundreds of balls are given from Jan. to Feb., often 40 of them a night during its height. The first is the Kaiserball in the Hofburg on New Year's Eve, but the greatest and the most glittering is the Opern-ball in the Opera; white tie and grand gala evening gown are the requirements here.

Other top balls are Philharmonikerball in the Wiener Musikverein building, Campagnereiterball (Riding Club) in Pallavicini Palace, and Jägerball (Hunter's Ball) all of them very exclusive: invitations, and, of course, formal attire are needed; at the Jägerball you can only wear a festive dirndl and a salon-type of Styrian hunting suit.

There is a wide variety of other balls from those organized by various university departments, intellectual clubs, and artists to the informal dances of plumbers and chimney-sweeps. Vienna Fasching season is much more formal than its Munich and Cologne counterparts. You might also find yourself at a *Gschnas*—a fancy-dress ball. Many coffee-houses are open from the small hours to serve beer and gulasch-soup to weary party-goers on their way home.

February is usually the month for skiing in Vienna's outskirts and, together with Jan., the month of ice skating competitions.

March brings the Spring Trade Fair and the Viennale, a film festival of growing importance.

Art exhibits are often concentrated in **April,** which also marks the start of a long series of conventions. The first of the outdoor restaurants open.

Heurigers begin mushrooming with the warmer **May** weather.

The most prominent summer event is the Festival of Vienna, which takes place annually during May–June. There is a series of performances in all Vienna theaters, and a series of concerts given by famous local and foreign orchestras, choirs, and soloists in the various halls of Musikverein and Konzerthaus, as well as in several other palaces and gardens.

Palace and park concerts (including those in the Rathaus and Schön-brunn Palace), and operetta performances at the Staatsoper and Volksoper continue through **July** and **August,** which are the best months for Danube trips. Check for concert or opera performances by the Haydn Sinfonietta in the Redoutensaal of the Hofburg.

The Autumn Trade Fair is the feature of **Sept.** when the principal theaters re-open their doors. Others stay open all the year.

Grape harvests and wine tasting **Oct.;** this is also the month to get that pheasant—at least garnished with dumplings and cranberries.

Opera runs from **Sept.** 1 to June 30, with various high points, but closing only on Good Friday, Christmas Eve, and one night before and the night of the Opera Ball.

Some of the best church music can be heard in **Dec.,** at the end of which Vienna, with the Strauss introduction played by the Philharmoniker at their traditional Dec. 31 and **Jan.** 1 concerts, plunges with music in her heart into the New Year. Now equally traditional, the Vienna Symphony performs Beethoven's Ninth Symphony on both dates in the Konzerthaus.

SIGHTSEEING TOURS. Apart from the museums and galleries, the parks and gardens, all of which can be visited at your own speed, there are plenty of organized tours to introduce you to the city and its surroundings.

Wiener Rundfahrten (Vienna Sightseeing Tours), Stelzhammergasse 4, offer twice daily (in summer three times a day) sightseeing tours of the city, Kahlenberg and Klosterneuburg, and Heiligenkreuz, Mayerling and Baden; one-hour tours, 10 and 11.30 A.M., departure from the Opera.

Vienna by Night tours are operated by the same firm, as well as by a number of travel agencies offering sightseeing tours: *Cosmos,* Kärntnerring 15; *Cityrama Sightseeing,* Scholzgasse 10.

Vienna Walks, lasting up to 90 minutes, are guided walks that give you the chance to explore unknown Vienna. A monthly leaflet of planned walks is available from the Tourist Office. For details, tel. 74 52 02, 220 66 20 or 93 90 88.

On selected days at 2 P.M., a party leaves the Café Landtmann by the Burgtheater on a guided walk through the 1st. district, lasting about 2½ hours. German, English and Spanish commentary (32 46 774).

On summer Saturdays at 2.30, Sundays and holidays at 10 A.M., there is a special trip around the Ring, to Belvedere, Prater and Schönbrunn with an old-timer (1909) trolley. Departures from Karlsplatz. Get tickets in advance from the Stadtwerke Information office underneath, Mon.–Fri. 7 A.M.–6 P.M., Sat., Sun. and holidays 8.30 A.M.–4 P.M., AS150 for the two-hour trip, children AS50. Book early, as the trip is frequently sold out in advance. Any remaining tickets either at the office or on the tram. Information tel. 587 51 89, 587 31 86.

If you long to visit the sewers made famous by the *Third Man,* visits for parties of 20 people can be arranged on certain days. Tel. 42800–2950 for information.

Buses to nearby areas in Lower Austria leave from *Österreichisches Verkehrsbüro* (Austrian tourist agency), Friedrichstr 7, and from *Austrobus,* Opernpassage, for Mayerling and the Vienna Woods.

From April to Oct. the *Danube Steamship Company* (DDSG) provides sightseeing boat trips along the Danube Canal and the main Danube stream within the city limits. The starting point is at Schwedenbrücke on the Canal.

The caves at Hinterbrühl near Vienna, which were used during the war for the production of the Heinkel jet fighters, can now be visited; here also is the largest (6,200 square meters) underground lake in Europe.

VIENNA FROM A TO Z. All buildings of historic interest are marked by explanatory shields (in summer festooned with red-white banners); a guide in English called *Vienna from A to Z* to these shields can be bought for AS30 in the Vienna Information Office, Kärntnerstr. 38, or in most bookstores.

In most churches of importance there are coin-operated (AS 10) tape machines which will give you an excellent commentary on the history and architecture of the building in English.

SPANISH RIDING SCHOOL. A unique attraction of Vienna are the performances of the Spanish Riding School in Hofburg's Baroque and chandeliered manège. Courbettes, levades, and caprioles are performed to the sounds of Mozart's music. The white stallions, called Lippizaner (until 1918 the stud farm was in Lippiza near Trieste, at that time within the borders of Austria; now it is at Piber in Styria) are trained according to the classical method.

Most performances take place on Sunday mornings (10.45) and Wednesday evenings (7) from March to June and September to November. From mid-April through June, in September and October there are extra shortened half-hour performances on Saturdays at 9 in the morning. Performances are now also held in July and August. During summer occasional performances are held in the gardens of Schönbrunn in the evening; ask about details.

Tickets *must* be booked in advance, and reservations should be made as early as possible. Tickets for Sunday performances may be obtained from the *Spanische Reitschule,* Hofburg, 1010 Vienna. Reservations for Wednesday and shortened Saturday performances handled by ticket offices and travel agents *only.*

The training sessions can be visited from February to June, September till November, every day except Sunday and Monday, 10–12. Visits to the stables are possible, although days and times are not fixed. Check at the stable entrance.

MUSEUMS AND GALLERIES. At present there are over 50 museums and galleries in Vienna. Entrance charges are minimal; for extensive museum visiting, a "Museum Pass" can be bought for AS150—it is very good value as you can use it to gain admission to 39 museums, at any time of day. On the first Sunday of the month admission is usually free; small charge for guided tours. Always study the posters for current special exhibitions.

Important Note. Visiting hours differ from museum to museum and also in some cases between the winter period (Oct. 1 to April 30) and the summer period (May 1 to Sept. 30). Alas, these hours are anything but fixed and can change literally from day to day. With this in mind check carefully before setting out on a museum crawl. There are few things worse than being faced by a closed door with no chance to return when it's open. For information about times call 43 16 08 from 9 A.M. to 7 P.M.

Akademie der Bildenden Künste (Gallery of the Academy of Fine Arts), 1010, Schillerplatz 3 (58 8 16–0). Upstairs from the main entrance to the Academy. About 150 paintings, among them Hieronymus Bosch, Titian, Cranach, Rubens, Rembrandt, Van Dyck. Tues., Thurs. and Fri. 10–2; Wed. 10–1 and 3–6; Sat., Sun. and holidays 9–1.

Albertina, 1010, Augustinerstr. 1 (53 4 83–0). Magnificent collection of graphic arts. Mon., Tues., Thurs. 10–4; Wed. 10–6; Fri. 10–2; Sat., Sun. 10–1. Closed on holidays and Sun. in July/August. Jan.–Feb., special show featuring noted architect Adolf Loos.

Arsenal (Army Museum), 1030, Arsenalstr. (78 23 03). Mon. to Thurs. 10–4; Sat., Sun. 10–4.

Beethoven Museums. Beethoven-Haus, 1190, Probusgasse 6. **Beethoven Apartment,** 1060, Laimgrubengasse 22, where Beethoven lived from 1822–23. **Eroica House,** 1190, Döblinger Hauptstr. 92. Where he composed his 3rd Symphony. **Pasqualati House,** 1010, Mölker Bastei 8. Memorial rooms. All are open May to Sept., Tues. to Sun. 10–12.15 and 1–4.30.

Belvedere (Unteres), Lower Belvedere, The Baroque Musuem, 1030, Rennweg 6 (78 41 58–0). Tues. to Sun. 10–4.

Belvedere (Oberes), Upper Belvedere, 1030, Prinz Eugen Str. 27. Austrian Gallery; works by Klimt, Schiele, Kokoschka, Romanko and Biedermeier painters. Tues. to Sun. 10–4.

Bestattungsmuseum (Funeral Museum), 1040, Goldeggasse 19 (501 95/227). Collection of material connected with funerals. Open Mon. to Fri. 12–3 on request.

Bundessammlung alter Stilmöbel, 1070, Mariahilfstr. 88 (93 42 40–99). Collection of period furniture. Guided tours. Tues. to Fri. 9–4; Sat. 9–12.

Dom- und Diözesanmuseum, Erzbishöfliches Palais, 1010, Stephansplatz 6 (51 5 52–0). Cathedral and religious material, plus the 1365 portrait of Rudolf IV of Habsburg, a very early work. Wed. to Sat. 10–4; Sun. 10–1.

Ephesos Museum, 1010, Heldenplatz in the Neue Burg (93 45 41). Material from the excavations at Ephesus. Mon./Wed./Fri. 10–4, Sat. 9–4.

Fiaker Museum, 1170, Veronikagasse 12 (43 88 52). History of the Viennese horse cab. 1st Wed. of the month, 10–1.

Freud Haus, 1090, Berggasse 19 (31 15 96). Where Sigmund Freud lived and worked, 1891–1938. Mon. to Fri. 9–1; Sat., Sun. 9–3.

Glockenmuseum, 1100, Troststr. 38 (604 34 60). Private collection of bells. Open Wed. 2–5.

Haydn Museum, 1060, Haydngasse 19 (596 13 07). Haydn's apartment; one room commemorates Brahms. Tues. to Sun. 10–12.15 and 1–4.30.

Historisches Museum der Stadt Wien, 1040, Karlsplatz 30 (505 87 47). Excellent survey of Vienna's history, imaginatively displayed. Tues. to Sun. 9–4.30. Special shows this year feature the architect Adolf Loos, *Art in Prague ca. 1400,* Egon Schiele, and *Living in Vienna.*

Hermes Villa, 1130, Lainzer Tiergarten, access Hermesstr (84 13 24). Small palace built for the Empress Elizabeth; used for temporary exhibitions. (See also under *Parks and Gardens,* Lainzer Tiergarten.) Wed. to Sun. 9–4.30. This year's exhibits offer *Rudolf, a Life in the Shadow of Mayerling* (through Feb.) and *Discover—Cover Up, the Art of Seduction* (from Apr.).

Herzgruft, in the Augustinerkirche, Augustinerstr. 3. The "Heart Crypt" where the Habsburg hearts lie in silver caskets. Open on request (533 09 47).

Hoftafel- und Silberkammer, 1010, Hofburg, Michaelertrakt, (93 42 40–99), entrance just inside the Michaelertor, under the dome. Court silverware and porcelain. Tues. to Fri. and Sun. 9–1.

Josefinum (History of Medicine Museum), 1090, Währingerstr. 25 (43 21 54). Display of wax anatomy figures; development of the Vienna School of Medicine. Mon. to Fri. 11–3.

Kaisergruft, 1010, Neuer Markt (512 68 53). Burial place of the Habsburgs. Oct. to April, daily 9.30–12; May to Sept., daily 9.30–4.

Kunsthistorisches Museum, (Museum of Art History), 1010, Burgring 5 (93 45 41). One of the world's greatest artistic treasurehouses. Tues. to Fri. 10–6 (in summer Tues. and Fri. 10–9); Sat. and Sun. 9–6. Closed Mon.

Kunstlerhaus, 1010, Karlsplatz 5 (587 96 63). Daily 9–5, but hours may vary. May–June, *Vienna School of Fantastic Realism;* Dec.–summer 1991, *Mozart and His Era.*

Mozart Erinnerungsräume, 1010, Domgasse 5 (Figarohaus) (513 62 94). Mozart's apartment, where he is said to have spent his happiest years. Tues. to Sun. 10–12.15 and 1–4.30.

Museum des 20. Jahrhunderts (Museum of the 20th Century), 1030, Schweizer Garten (78 25 50–0). Close to the Südbahnhof. Modern art special exhibitions. Daily 10–6, except Wed.

Museum für Angewandte Kunst (Museum of Applied Arts), 1010, Stubenring 5 (711 36 0). A slightly disappointing collection of applied arts. Thurs. to Mon. 11–6.

Museum Moderner Kunst (Museum of Modern Art), 1090, Fürstengasse 1, in former Palais Liechtenstein (34 12 59). Incongruous mixture of magnificent rooms and the latest trends in art; some superb works, but patchy. Daily 10–6; closed Tues. Handy cafe.

Museum für Völkerkunde (Ethnological Museum), 1010, Heldenplatz (93 45 41). Huge collection of material from all over the world and many ages. Tues. to Fri. 9–4.

Museum für Volkskunde (Folklore Museum), 1080, Laudongasse 15–19 (43 89 05–0). Peasant art, furniture and crafts. Tues. to Fri. 9–3; Sat. 9–12; Sun. 9–1.

Nationalbibliothek (National Library), 1010, Josefsplatz 1 (534 10/245). The great Baroque central hall of the library, a cathedral of books—the Prunksaal. May to Oct., Mon. to Sat. 10–4 and Nov. to Apr., Mon. to Sat. 11–12. Special exhibits this year feature Italian Gothic and Renaissance book illustration (mid-May to mid-Oct.), and *Mozart and Salieri* (from Dec.).

Naturhistorisches Museum (Natural History Museum), 1010, Burgring 7 (93 45 41). All you could ever want to know about the animal kingdom (stuffed), rocks, early artifacts (including the Willendorf Venus), etc. Open daily 9–6. Closed Tues.

Niederösterreichisches Landesmuseum (Museum of Lower Austria), 1010, Herrengasse 9 (531 10 0). The landscape and culture of the area around Vienna. Tues. to Fri. 9–5; Sat. 9–2; Sun. 9–12.

Neue Galerie, i.d. Stallburg. 1010, Reitschulg 2. (533 60 45). Wed. to Mon., 10–4.

Planetarium, 1020, PraterHauptallee (near the Giant Wheel) (24 94 32). Sat., Sun. 3 and 5. Special performances for groups. In the same building, a museum of relics from the old Prater.

Schatzkammer (The Hofburg Treasury), 1010, Hofburg, Schweizerhof (93 45 41, weekends 93 44 48). A uniquely magnificent collection of the Habsburg crown jewels. Opening hours Mon., Wed. to Fri. 10–6; Sat. to Sun. 9–6.

Schatzkammer des Deutschen Ordens (Treasury of the Teutonic Knights), 1010, Singerstr. 7, (512 10 65). Daily 10–12; Tues., Wed., Fri. and Sat. 3–5.

Schloss Schönbrunn (Palace of Schönbrunn), 1130, Schönbrunner Schlosstr. (83 36 46). Guided tours only. **Wagenburg** (Carriage museum, closed Mon.) attached. Oct. to April daily 9–12, 1–4; May to Sept. daily 9–12, 1–5. **Gloriette,** daily 8–6. **Zoo,** daily 9–6.

Schubert Museums. Schuberts Geburtshaus, 1090, Nussdorferstr. 54 (34 59 924). Schubert's birthplace, a nice old Biedermeier building. Tues. to Sun. 10–12.15 and 1–4.30. **Schuberts Sterbehaus,** 1040, Kettenbrückengasse 6 (57 39 072). The house where Schubert died. Tues. to Fri. 10–4; Sat. 2–6; Sun. 9–1.

Johann Strauss Apartment, 1020, Praterstr. 54 (24 01 21). Birthplace of the *Blue Danube.* Tues. to Fri. 10–4; Sat. 2–6; Sun. 9–1.

Tabak Museum (Tobacco Museum), in Messepalast, Mariahilferstr. entrance (96 17 16). Tues. 10–5, Wed. to Fri., 10–3, Sat. and Sun., 9–1.

Technisches Museum (Technical Museum), 1150, Mariahilferstr. 212 (83 36 18). Tues. to Fri. 9–4; Sat. 9–1; Sun. 9–4. The first typewriter, among other treasures.

Theater Museum, 1010, Lobkowitzpl., in Palais Lobkowitz (512 24 27). In magnificent new quarters, with excellent rotating exhibitions from the (unseen) vast collection of theater memorabilia. Tues. to Sat., 10–5, Sun., 9–1.

Tramway Museum, 1030, Erdbergstr. 109 (712 12 01). Museum of old Viennese streetcars. May to Sept. Sat., Sun., holidays 9–4.

Uhrenmuseum (Clock Museum), 1010, Schulhof 2 (533 22 65). 3,000 clocks from many periods. Tues. to Sun. 9–12.15, 1–4.30.

Otto Wagner Apartment, 1070, Doblerg. 4. (93 22 33). The architect responsible for Vienna's "Jugendstil" (art nouveau) movement. Open Mon. to Fri. 9–12.

Wine Museum Döbling, 1190, Döblinger Hauptstr. 96 (36 10 042). Sat. 3.30–6; Sun. 10–12.

Zirkus und Clownmuseum, 1020, Karmelitergasse 9 (34 68 15). Museum tracing the development and history of the circus in Vienna. Wed. 5.30–7; Sat. 2.30–5; Sun. 9–12.

PARKS AND GARDENS. The average Viennese loves to do most of his warm-weather walking in the **Wienerwald** (Vienna Woods), romantic locale of Johann Strauss' famous waltz and of many a song and poem. The Wienerwald is not a park, but a range of low, wooded hills, crisscrossed by pathways and roads and framing Vienna on the western side. Among Vienna parks proper the visitor has a wide selection through which to stroll. Bus lines 10A, 39A and 38A will land you on the edge of the woods, as will 49B and 52B.

Belvedere Park. The main part between Lower and Upper Belvedere and a smaller part with an artificial lake between Upper Belvedere and Südbahnhof. Formally laid out in Italian terrace style. Many garden sculptures, wrought-iron gateway by Arnhold and Konrad Küffner made in 1728. Two main entrances, Rennweg 6 or Prinz Eugenstr. 27—both within easy reach of the center. Take the streetcar D marked Südbahnhof up the Prinz Eugen Str. to the Upper Belvedere.

Botanischer Garten, Rennweg 14, also next to Belvedere (the other side), is part of Museum of the Botanical Institute of the University; admission to the garden April 15–Oct. 1, 9 A.M. till dusk. Many rare plants. Permission from superintendent to visit interesting hot-houses.

Burggarten. A small, lovely park next to Neue Hofburg. Mozart Monument, statue of Emperor Franz Josef. On the Burgring.

Donauinsel. Has its own stop on the U1, on the Reichsbrücke. A natural leisure park on a 14-mile island between the two banks of the Danube. All facilities, beaches, walkways, and sunbathing, nude in designated areas.

Donaupark, Arbeiterstrandbadgasse, take the U1 as far as Alte Donau. Danube Park, laid out between the Danube and the so-called Old Danube for the International Garden Show of 1964. One of its most outstanding features is the 826-foot observation tower (Donauturm) with a rotating café-restaurant offering a magnificent view. There are several other cafés and restaurants.

Lainzer Tiergarten. Take streetcar 62 (Lainz) from diagonally opposite the Opera, change to bus 60B (Lainzer Tor), or take the U4 from Karlsplatz to Hütteldorf. A natural game park, formerly imperial game preserve, with deer, boar, and even mouflon, similar to the Rocky Mountain bighorn. The park is very large and it takes several hours to walk across it. In the middle is the Hermes Villa, built originally in the 19th century for the Empress Elisabeth and used today for exhibitions. There is a delightful restaurant at the Villa, indoor and outdoor eating, with good food at reasonable prices. Cars and other vehicles are not allowed and one must walk only along marked paths. There are several entrances. Open 8 A.M. until 1 hour before dusk, April 1 to Oct. 31. Closed Mon. and Tues.

Prater. Subway U1 from Karlsplatz to Praterstern. Very large natural park area (over 10 square km. altogether), once hunting grounds and pleasure park of the emperor, opened to public as early as second half of 18th century. At present includes various sports establishments (stadium, swimming pool, golf course, race track, etc.), Trade Fair exhibition area, and so-called Volksprater. Latter is actually an elaborate amusement park with the famous giant Ferris Wheel as an outstanding feature and several taverns, cafés, dancehalls inside and nearby. Particularly crowded on Sun. afternoons. It has been considerably restored and rejuvenated over the last two years.

Schönbrunn Park. Take subway U4 to Schönbrunn station and walk forward, or one more stop to Hietzing and walk back. A formally laid-out park in Baroque style belonging to Schönbrunn Palace. The Neptun Brunnen and Schöne Brunnen fountains, which gave the palace its name; Gloriette, a colonnade from the top of which there is a beautiful view of the entire Schönbrunn area and beyond; Zoo, Botanical Garden, Palm House, Tiroler Garten, carriage museum and magnificent Baroque theater.

Stadtpark. Along the Park Ring, with small artificial lake, various statues—among them one of Franz Schubert and the famous one of Johann Strauss. Bandstandmusic late afternoons and evenings in summer.

Türkenschanzpark. Next to School of Agriculture, bus 40A from the corner of Schottenring and Liechtensteinstr. The largest rambling wooded variety of park in the city, located on site where Turks built their fortification during siege of Vienna, hence the name.

Volksgarten. Next to Burgtheater, on site of old city wall fortifications. Several monuments, including an attractive one to the Empress Elisabeth and another to the author/playwright Grillparzer. Theseus Temple, occasionally used for exhibitions, and Tilgner Fountain with bronze fauns and nymphs. Refresh yourself in the company of the Austrian government at the delightful Cafe Meierei close to the Ballhausplatz entrance. Reasonable prices and good food and drink.

ENTERTAINMENT. Vienna is one of the main performing arts centers of the German-speaking world . . . indeed, where music is concerned of the world *tout simple*. Which is lucky for most visitors who may have trouble coming to grips with the latest and avant-garde production of a play by an unknown Serbo-Croat intellectual. Indeed, even Shakespeare in an "updated" version may appear in virtually unrecognizable shape, and classics closer to home have been known to suffer similar self-indulgent productions. But with music, and opera especially, the Viennese do not take excessive liberties.

Opera. The main opera house (51 4 44–0) and one of the world's greatest, is the **Staatsoper.** With a pre-season beginning in Sept. and the Festival in June, opera performances go on continuously from Sept. 1 to end June. There is also a new policy of operetta performances here during July and Aug. given by the Volksoper company. The yearly program represents a happy selection from different periods and composers, unlike some world opera houses which tailor their programs to the nationality of their singers. Evening dress and black tie are not compulsory, but they are recommended for first performances and for better seats. Jeans—even designer ones—are frowned upon, even in standing room. In Vienna, opera is a dressy event.

Operas of a lighter type and operettas are presented at the **Volksoper,** a bit out, on the corner of Gürtel and Währingerstr (take streetcar 41, 42 or 43 from "downstairs" at Schottentor on the Ring), but which is significantly cheaper than the Opera. Thus the tradition of Johann Strauss and Franz Lehar is continuing in the city that gave them their great successes.

Operettas and musical shows are also performed at **Theater an der Wien,** Linke Wienzeile 6 and at the newly renovated **Raimundtheater,** 1060, Wallgasse 18, and at the **Ronacher,** 1010, Seilerstätte/ Himmelpfortgasse.

In summer, some chamber opera performances are given in the **Schlosstheater** of Schönbrunn. Chamber opera is also planned for the **Redoutensaal** of the Hofburg.

Drama. Large posters all over town give up-to-the-minute information concerning all theaters. Visitors with sufficient command of the German language should take advantage of the unique attraction offered by Vienna in the field of dramatic arts at the **Burgtheater.** Vienna is one of the leading centers in the cultivation of German theatrical arts and for a German-language actor to play at the Burg means supreme achievement. Closed in summer.

Thanks to this tradition, it is logical that there are many other drama theaters in the city. Among the most important are—**Akademietheater,** Lisztstr. 1 (next to the Konzerthaus), this is the small house of the Burgtheater, classical and modern plays; **Theater in der Josefstadt,** Josefstädterstr. 26, the old theater of Max Reinhardt, classical and modern plays; **Volkstheater,** Neustiftgasse 1, dramas, comedies, folk plays; **Kammerspiele,** Rotenturmstr. 20, modern plays.

There are also a number of small theaters, such as the new **Künstlerhaus, Atelier Theater am Naschmarkt, Theater der Courage,** and **Tribüne.**

Simpl, Wollzeile 36, has a long tradition of poking fun at Austrian and world politics and life in general, but this type of entertainment calls for knowledge of local affairs and dialect.

The **Vienna English Theater,** Josefsgasse 12, 1080 (42 12 60) offers mainly standard pieces in English, featuring the occasional star to supplement the local company. Equally good is the **International Theater,** 1090, Porzellangasse 8 (31 62 72), also performing in English.

Music. The two great orchestras of the capital are the **Vienna Philharmonic** and the **Vienna Symphony.** In addition to their performances, there is an abundance of concerts by soloists, choruses, and chamber music groups.

The most important concert halls in Vienna are in the building of the **Gesellschaft der Musikfreunde** (popularly called *Musikverein*), Dumbastr. 3, the home of the Vienna Philharmonic, and in the **Wiener Konzerthaus,** Lothringerstr. 20. Both of these contain several auditoriums for concerts of different types, and your ticket may be marked with the name of the particular hall in which the concert is being given. Don't hunt vainly for a building with that name. If your ticket is for the **Grosser Musikvereinssaal,** the **Brahmssaal** or the **Kammersaal,** go to the **Musikfreunde** building. If it is for the **Grosser Konzerthaussaal,** the **Mozartsaal** or the **Schubertsaal,** you will find it in the **Konzerthaus.**

Concerts are also given in the small **Figarosaal** of the Palffy Palace, the concert studio of the broadcasting station in **Argentinierstrasse** and the **Bösendorfersaal** of the famous piano manufacturer.

In addition to the Vienna Festival, held late-May and June, there are special summer concerts in the Arkadenhof (Arcade Court) of the Rathaus, in Belvedere garden and Volksgarten, and in many palaces, the most notable being held in Palais Schwarzenberg, Schloss Schönbrunn; but of particular interest are the Mozart concerts given in 18th-century costumes and powdered wigs in the Konzerthaus and the Sofiensäle.

Schubert fans can enjoy occasional piano concerts in the house of his birth, Nussdorferstr. 54.

Church music of high artistic value can be heard during Sunday morning Mass in the following churches in the downtown area—in the Cathedral of St. Stephen, in the Franciscan Church and, above all, in the Augustinerkirche.

Perhaps the most famous of these locales is the Hofburgkapelle where the famous **Wiener Sängerknaben** (Vienna Choirboys) sing at 9.15 A.M. from mid-Sept. to late June. Written ticket reservations for seats (standing room is free) should be made at least eight weeks in advance to: *Hofmusikkapelle Hofburg,* A-1010 Vienna. You will then get a reservation card, which you present to the box office of the Burgkapelle when you pick up and pay for your tickets. A separate contingent of tickets is sold at the box office of the Burgkapelle every Friday from 5 P.M. onwards. It is advisable to queue early (from about 4.30)! A maximum of two tickets per person may be purchased from the box office (tickets also available in ticket and travel agencies, but with a service charge added). Programs published on first of month on church door and in the Saturday papers. There are Wednesday evening organ concerts in St. Stephen's from early May to end Nov.

Try to hear brass band music on various squares and in different parks.

You can hear excellent live jazz at the following: **Jazzland,** 1010, Franz Josefskai 29 (63 25 75), Tues. to Sat. 9 P.M. to 2 A.M.; **Jazzspelunke,** 1060, Dürergasse 3 (587 01 26); **Miles Smiles,** 1080, Lange Gasse 51 (42 84 814); **Opus One,** 1010 Mahlerstr. 11 (513 20 75) to 4 A.M.; **Papa's Tapas,** 1040, Schwarzenbergplatz 10 (65 03 11) from 10 P.M. daily; and **Rotor Engel,** 1010, Rabensteig 5 (535 41 05).

Enquire at your hotel about coffeehouses presenting live music. There is an increasing number.

Getting Tickets. Operas are almost always, and better concerts usually, sold out in Vienna, so it is advisable to buy your tickets several days in advance.

For State theaters (Oper, Volksoper, Akadamietheater, and Burgtheater) you can get tickets in the city ticket office located in a courtyard near the Opera, with entrances from Goethegasse 1 and Hanuschgasse 3, as well as at the individual theaters.

The sale of tickets begins one week in advance for the State theaters, but the tickets may be sold out a couple of hours after the sale is open (people begin waiting in line several hours earlier). Tickets, if any remain, can also be purchased within one hour before the beginning of the performance at the evening ticket office of the theater concerned. You can order tickets by phone, charging them to a credit card (AE, DC, MC, V), up to six days before the performance, by calling (0222) 513 15 13. Credit cards also accepted at the ticket office. Tickets for theaters other than the four mentioned can be purchased during the daily business hours 8 to 10 days ahead or within one hour before the performance at the respective theater ticket office. Sale of tickets for special events starts earlier; for the New Year's Concert it starts on Dec. 17.

For opera and operetta performances write about 2 or 3 months in advance to the nearest Austrian National Tourist Office in the U.S., Canada or the U.K. to get a list of the coming performances and special blank order forms. Then send an order form duly filled in—but no money—to the ticket office Bundestheaterverband, Goethegasse 1, 1010 Vienna. When you get to Vienna, take the reservation card you will receive to that address and pick up and pay for your tickets.

You can buy tickets also at the various ticket agencies and, even more important, particularly for the opera, you can order tickets from them in advance and they will see to it that you get them. The fee charged by the agencies is generally 20% of the ticket price (hotel porters usually charge more) but most of these organizations have a tendency to ignore the existence of cheap seats. Budget tourists would do well to go to the city ticket office themselves.

MOVIES. After a period of neglect, cinemas have come back into fashion in Vienna and many have been converted into multi-auditoria cinecenters. Both the variety and quality of presentation—to say nothing of the comfort—have improved enormously. As most movie houses show films dubbed into German, these two should interest the visitor—the **Burgkino,** at Opernring 19, which shows films of artistic merit in the original language (mostly English); and the **de France kino** on the Schottenring which presents new releases in English only. The **Top Kino** on the Gumpendorferstrasse also presents new releases in English, and the **Filmmuseum** in the Albertina shows older films in the original language, the majority of which are in English.

NIGHTLIFE. Although there are a fair number of night spots in Vienna, the city cannot boast a real nightclub tradition. The average Viennese prefers to go to the opera, theater, and concerts for serious entertainment, and for a relaxed evening, out to dinner or to a wine tavern or Heuriger. The Viennese love to dance, but the dancing is done mostly at the numerous balls during the season, in a few cafes with weekend music, and in dance-bars.

Nightclubs with floor shows are to be avoided in Vienna: they are generally expensive and bad. Having warned you, the following places are the best in town: **Casanova,** Dorotheerg. 6 (512 98 45), open till 4 A.M. DC, MC, V; **Moulin-Rouge,** Walfischg 11 (512 21 30), open 10 P.M.–6A.M.; closed Sun. DC, MC, V.

The leading night spots for dancing are: **Eden-Bar,** Liliengasse 2, near St. Stephen's, (512 74 50), open 10 P.M.–4A.M. AE, DC, MC, V; **Splendid Bar,** Jasomirgottstr. 3 (533 15 15), open till 4 A.M. AE, DC, MC, V; **Fledermaus,** Spiegelgasse 2 (512 84 38). A mixture of literary cabaret and soul singing or whatever else is available; closed Sun. and Mon. DC.

What Vienna does have is innumerable, delightful and quite sophisticated bars. Here are just four suggestions, for a walk along the Rotenturmstr, Räbensteig/Judengasse ("Bermuda Triangle"), Bäckerstr, Schönlaternstr. area will present you with numerous choices: **Chamäleon,** Blutgasse 3 (513 17 03); **Galerie Bar,** 1010, Singerstr. 7 (512 49 29), AE, MC.

Portas, Schulerstr. 6; **Reiss-Bar,** 1010, Marco d'Avianogasse 1, open till 2 A.M.

Other dance bars and discos include—**Atrium,** Schwarzenbergplatz 10
(65 35 94). Popular with students, and boasting 50 types of beer; a disco.
Closed Sun. and Mon.

Casino Cercle Wien, Kärntnerstrasse 41 (512 48 36), for blackjack, rou-
lette and gambling in a former palace.

Chatanooga, Graben 29 (533 50 00), with the accent on youth and jazz;
live music.

Lords Club, Karlsplatz 1 (505 83 08). Occasional live shows.

Magic, in the Volksgarten (63 05 18).

Queen Anne, Johannesgasse 12 (512 02 03).*The* hottest disco in town.

Schwimmende Pyramide, Seilerstätte 5.

Scotch, Parkring 10, chic (512 94 17).

Take Five, Annagasse 3A, open 10 A.M.–4 A.M.

Tenne, Annagasse 3 (512 57 08). Occasional live shows.

Wake Up Disco Club, Seilerstätte 5.

SHOPPING. The finest shops in Vienna line Kärntnerstrasse from the
Opera to St. Stephen's Cathedral, then run left through the Graben and
again left, following Kohlmark to the Imperial Palace. Almost all the
small side streets within and adjoining this roughly outlined square form
part of one of the best shopping districts in Europe. Part of this area is
now a pedestrian precinct, with cafés in the open air in summer.

See *Planning Your Trip* for details of how to recover Value Added Tax.

Vienna's Flea Market, with everything from junk to fine antiques, is
next to the market area at Kettenbrückengasse, 1050, every Sat., 8–6, not
on public holidays. A "quality" flea market operates Sat. and Sun. 2–8
in summer alongside the Danube Canal below Schwedenbrücke.

The following list is of shops dealing with typically Austrian merchan-
dise.

Austrian Jade. *Burgenland,* Opernpassage 4, and Wildpretmarkt 6, AE.

Books. *British Bookshop,* Weihburggasse 8; *Heidrich's,* Plankengasse 7;
Pickwick's, Marc-Aurel-Str. 10–12; *Shakespeare & Co,* Sterngasse 2.

Candles. *Metzger.* Stephansplatz 7; *Jos. Altmann,* Heidenschuss 1 and
Mariahilferstr. 51, 1060. AE. *Marius Retti,* Kohlmarkt 8–10. AE.

Ceramics. *Krolop* (Gmunden ceramics), Kärntnerdurchgang; a few
shops around the corner from Kärntnerstr. 10, AE. *Pawlata,* Kärntnerstr.
14. AE.

Crystal. *Bakalowits,* Spiegelgasse 3; *Lobmeyr,* Kärntnerstr. 26. Best
crystal, tableware and gift articles—they made the crystal glass chandeliers for New York's Metropolitan Opera. AE, DC.

Dirndls and Trachten for Women. *Lanz,* Kärntnerstr. 10, AE, DC, MC;
Tostmann, Schottengasse 3A, AE, DC, MC, V; *Loden-Plankl,* Michaelerplatz
6, AE; *Modell-Dirndl,* Tegetthofstr. 6, AE, DC; *Resi Hammerer,* Kärntnerstr.
29–31, AE, DC, MC, V.

Glass. *Table-Top,* in exclusive Freyung Arcade in Palais Ferstel. Specialist in exquisite hand-blown Riedel glass. DC.

Handicrafts, Gifts and Souvenirs. *Österreichische Werkstätten,* Kärntnerstr. 6, AE, MC; *Souvenir in der Hofburg,* Hofburg Arcade, AE, MC; *Boutique Gretl,* Bognergasse 7, especially for enamel clocks, AE; *Niederösterreichisches Heimatwerk,* Herrengasse 6–8, AE, DC, MC, V; *Tiroler Werkkunst,*
Mariahilferstr. 89, 1060, AE.

Hats. *Collins Hüte,* Opernpassage; *P & C Habig,* 1040, Wiedner Hauptstr. 15 (65 81 04) AE, DC, V. Note the superb facade.

Jewelry. *A. Haban,* Kärntnerstr. 2, *the* Viennese spot for jewelry, on the corner of St. Stephen's Square, AE, DC, MC, V; *Heldwein,* Graben 13, AE, MC, V; *A. E. Köchert,* Neuer Markt 15, AE, DC, MC, V; *Paltscho,* Graben 14, AE, MC; *Jul. Hügler,* Freisingerstr. 4 and Kärntnerstr. 53, AE, DC; *Juwel,* Kohlmarkt 1, AE, DC, V; *Carius & Binder,* Kärntnerstr. 17, AE, DC, MC, V; *Horwath,* Kärntnerstr. 29–31, AE, DC, MC, V; *Kunz,* Neuer Markt 13, AE, DC, MC, V.

Ladies' Fashions. *Adlmüller,* Palais Esterhazy, Kärntnerstr. Couturier fashions at appropriate prices (also first-rate menswear). AE, DC, MC, V.

Men's Trachten. *Loden-Plankl,* Michaelerplatz 6, AE, DC, MC; *Collins Hüte,* Operngasse 12, for Alpine-style hats. MC, V.

Petit Point. *Berta Smejkal,* Opernpassage 13, Kohlmarkt 9, AE, V; *Stransky,* Hofburg-Passage 2.

Porcelain. *Augarten,* Schloss Augarten, 1060, Stock-im-Eisenplatz 3–4 and Mariahilferstr. 99, AE; *Ernst Wahliss,* Kärntnerstr. 17, AE, DC, MC; *Rasper & Söhne,* Graben 15, AE, DC, MC.

Wrought-iron and Weinhebers. *Horst Zach,* Habsburgergasse 5 and Bräunerstr. 8; *Hamerle,* Annagasse 7; *Reckzügel,* on the Stephansplatz.

RESTAURANTS. First class restaurants in Vienna can be quite expensive—for a full dinner, accompanied by a good bottle of wine, you will pay as much as in most other West European capitals. But in simpler restaurants, particularly in the suburbs, you can still find good food at refreshingly low prices. If you have your main meal at noon (as the Viennese do) you can take advantage of the luncheon specials.

There are still many traditional restaurants, but there has been a tremendous shake-up during the last five years, with many exciting new and high quality restaurants making their mark. Whatever you choose, you will have a relaxed evening, an experience that is difficult to come by in trendier towns.

Most restaurants serve meals only between 12 and 2.30, and between 6 and 10 or 11. An increasing number of restaurants stay open late serving after-theater dinners, but do reserve. Most are closed one day a week and holidays, and many take an annual vacation during July and August.

New bars and small restaurants are opening all the time and closing almost as fast. Many of them are very good, but it is not possible for us to keep track of them all. Check *Wien Wie es Isst,* an excellent comprehensive booklet available at any newsstand.

Expensive

Arche Noah, 1010, Seitenstettengasse 2 (533 13 74). High-class Kosher cooking near 18th-century Synagogue in the Old City. AE, DC, MC, V.

Astoria, 1010, Führichg. 1 (51 57 70). See *Hotels.* Paneled Jugendstil dining room. Excellent cooking, special after-theater set dinners. The best pianist in town. AE, DC, MC, V. Open late.

Balkan Grill, 1160, Brunnengasse 13 (92 14 94). Near West Station. Spicy Balkan specialties. Particular attraction is *Genghis Khan's Flaming Sword,* shashlik served flaming on a sword, with a musical flourish of Viennese and gypsy melodies. In summer an attractive garden. AE, DC, MC, V. Open late, closed Sun.

Csardasfürstin, 1010, Schwarzenbergstr. 2 (512 92 46). An old favorite, now in new hands. Gypsy music, Viennese concept of Hungarian food.

Da Conte, 1010, Kurrentgasse 12 (533 64 46). Small and romantic. Italian cuisine of a standard rare outside Italy. DC, MC, V. Closed Sun.

D'Rauchkuchl, 1150, Schweglerstr. 37 (92 13 81). Revitalized and back on top-form. Popular with celebrities. Closed Sun. evening. AE, DC, MC, V.

Drei Husaren, 1010, Weihburggasse 4 (512 10 92). Just off Kärntnerstr., near St. Stephen's. Candlelight, antique-style furnishings, soft piano music. Magnificent *hors d'oeuvres,* but watch prices! Very good selection of wines and first-class bar. Dinners only. Closes for 4 weeks July to Aug., and Sun. AE, DC, MC, V. Open late.

Four Seasons, Hotel Intercontinental (71122). New furnishings and a new cook have transformed this hotel restaurant into something special. AE, DC, MC, V.

Gottfried, 1030, Marxerg. 3 (73 82 56). Closed Sun., open late. AE, DC, MC, V.

Haas & Haas, 1010, Stephansplatz 4 (513–1916). Elegant snacks and dishes. Good wine. Beautiful shaded courtyard. Closed Sun.

Hauswirth, 1060, Otto Bauergasse 20 (587 12 61). In the 6th District, just off Mariahilferstr., with several large rooms and pleasant courtyard garden in summer. Go to the back room for piano music in the evening. Imaginative modern cooking. Closed Sun. AE, DC, MC, V.

Imperial, 1010, Kärntner Ring 16 (50 1 10–0). Good food and snacks available all day in café with coffee-house atmosphere. Gourmet dining of high quality in restaurant *Zur Majestät.* (501 10 356). Good drinks and music in the intimately arranged bar. Open late. AE, DC, MC, V.

Johanneshof, 1180, Gersthoferstr. 65, (47 83 24). Closed Sun. A Jugendstil jewel.

Kervansaray, 1010, Mahlerstr. 9 (512 88 43). Near the Opera. Turkish specialties, from *Kapama* to *Dönerkebab;* fresh fish from the Bosphorus, including lobsters flown in every day. Turkish décor, no music. Upstairs is a fish restaurant, *Hummer Bar,* which is very expensive—but worth it. Closed Sun. AE, DC, MC, V. Open late.

König von Ungarn, 1010, Schulerstr. 10 (512 53 19). Romantic, intimate setting. Attentive service. Some of the best boiled beef in town. Closed Sat. and August. AE, DC, MC, V.

Korso, Hotel Bristol, 1010, Kärntner Ring 1 (51 5 16–536). Beautifully-designed top gourmet restaurant. Exceptional wine list. AE, DC, MC, V.

Niky's Kuchlmasterei, 1030, Obere Weissgerberstr. 6 (72 44 18). Very good Viennese and French cooking in a pleasant, candlelit, rustic atmosphere. Open Mon. to Sat. 10 A.M. to midnight; closed Sun. and holidays. AE.

Palais Schwarzenberg, 1030, Schwarzenbergpl. 9 (78 45 15). See *Hotels.* In the small, but elegant dining room, there is much to revive belief in old Vienna. Excellent cuisine, wines and service. Stunning terrace overlooking private park. AE, DC, MC, V.

Prinz Eugen, 1030, Am Stadtpark (75 26 52). In the Hilton (see *Hotels*). Opulent surroundings provide a luxurious setting for excellent food. AE, DC, MC, V.

Sacher, 1010, Philharmonikerstr. 4 (512 33 67). See *Hotels.* The main restaurant sparkles as it did in the red-plush era of the Habsburgs, as do the alcoved dining rooms on the upper floor. One of the plusher spots to eat *Tafelspitz* (garnished boiled beef) and its own creation, *Sachertorte.* Open late. AE, DC, MC.

Sailer, 1180, Gersthoferstr. 14 (47 21 21). Near Türkenschanzpark. Modern Austrian specialties, marvelous wines. Paneled dining room, cellar and atmospheric garden in summer. Closed Sun., holidays. AE, DC, MC, V.

Schubert-Stüberl, 1010, Schreyvogelgasse 4 (63 71 87). Near Burgtheater; pleasant, with quiet summer garden; grill and game specialties. Closed Sun. AE, DC, MC, V. Open late.

Steinerne Eule, 1070, Halbgasse 30 (93 22 50). Gourmet restaurant with cozy little rooms. Closed Sun. and Mon. AE, DC, MC, V.

Steirereck, 1030, Rasumovskygasse 2 (73 31 68). On the Danube canal. Ranked among Vienna's best restaurants; lightly cooked Austrian dishes, with the emphasis on freshness. Superb wine list. Closed Sat. and Sun. and holidays. AE.

Moderate

Almhütte, 1090, Schlickgasse (31 67 50). Indigenous haunt of operetta stars. Simple well-cooked food. Excellent pianist Thurs., Fri. and Sat. Closed Sun. evening and all day Mon. MC, V.

Altes Haus, 1190, Himmelstr. 35 (32 23 21). In the wine-growing suburb of Grinzing, where every house is a wine tavern and this one is actually more a wine tavern with food than a restaurant in the proper sense. Try chicken, grilled and skewered meats, and *Topfenstrudl* (*strudl* made with cream cheese). Open evenings only, musical entertainment. Closed Sun. AE, DC, MC, V.

Basteibeisl, 1010, Stubenbastei 10 (512 43 19). Good Viennese cooking, old fashioned specialties. Friendly. Open Mon. to Sat. 9–12 P.M. AE, DC, MC, V.

Donauturm, 1022, Donauturmstr. 4 (23 53 68). On the second floor, at the top of the Danube Tower in Donaupark. Expensive international cuisine in the rotating tower; moderate cafe-restaurant on the lower floor (at 170 m. and 160 m.); rustic **Park Tavern** at foot of tower. AE, DC, V.

Dubrovnik, 1030, Am Heumarkt 5 (713 27 55). Excellent Balkan cooking and atmosphere. Open late. AE, DC, MC, V.

Eckel, 1190, Sieveringstr. 46 (32 32 18). Small house with wood paneled *stuben* and garden. Great cooking such as sweetwater crayfish (in season), trout, game, *Backhendl.* Fluffy, hot soufflé-type desserts such as *Pfannkuchen MarieLouise,* covered with chocolate sauce, ground nuts and whipped cream. A family-run establishment; closed Sun. and Mon. AE, DC, V.

Figlmüller, 1010, Wollzeile 5 (512 61 77). In historic courtyard. Folksy atmosphere. Giant schnitzels and excellent fruity wines from the Südbahn region. Closed Sat./Sun. and August. MC.

Gigerl, 1010, Rauhensteing. 3 (513 44 31). Good food and wine in newly restored house at the heart of Vienna's Old City. Open daily from 4 P.M. DC.

Glacisbeisl, 1070, Messepalast (96 16 58). Between the two museums on the Ring: hard to find, so ask the way. Sit out on what is left of medieval bastions. Excellent local cooking, friendly service. Closed Sun.

Gösser Bierklinik, 1010, Steindlgasse 4 (533 33 36). In a narrow street near Am Hof. One of the oldest inns in the city (1566) with numerous atmospheric rooms.

Himmelpforte, Himmelpfortg. 24 (513 19 66). "Schlemmerkeller" and bar. Excellent cooking and atmosphere. Reasonable. Open late Mon. to Sat. AE, DC, MC, V.

Ilona, 1010, Bräunerstr. 2 (512 61 91). Tiny, serving huge portions of Hungarian specialities. Closed Sun. DC, MC, V.

Johann Strauss, 1010 Schwedenplatz (533 61 33). Large old paddle-steamer beautifully restored and turned into restaurant, bar, café and dance floor. A treat in every way. Live jazz on Sunday mornings. Closed Sun. evening. AE, V.

Lucky Chinese, 1, Kärntnerstr. 24 (512 34 28). Good Chinese food. Open daily. AE, DC, MC, V.

Lugeck, 1010, Lugeck 7 (512 79 79). On the way from St. Stephen's to the Danube canal. Quick bite in the simpler ground-floor premises, more elaborate restaurant fare a few stairs below. AE, DC, MC, V.

Martinkovitz, 1190, Bellvuestr. 4 (32 15 46). Heuriger restaurant famous for its Backhendl. Good home grown wines. Closed Mon. and Tues.

Oswald & Kalb, 1010, Bäckerstr. 14 (512 13 71). Evenings only. Very popular with the young. Open daily and late.

Pastaron, 1010, Jasomirgottstr. 3 (535 55 44). Elegant, modern pasta restaurant of high standard. Good wines. Closed Sun., last orders 11.45.

Rathauskeller, 1010, Rathausplatz 1 (42 12 19). A vast establishment in the basement of the Rathaus (City Hall), with a series of vaulted dining rooms. Evenings, Viennese music in the large *Grinzingerkeller,* where a huge, carved, wooden barrel presides over long tables of tourists. Closed Sun. AE.

Rossini, Schönlaterngasse (52 62 14). Good Italian food. Closed Mon.

Siddartha, 1010, Fleischmarkt 16 (513 11 97). Sophisticated vegetarian spot. Dine healthily by candle-light, with organically grown wines. Delicious food—even for non-vegetarians. Reserve. Closed Sun.

S'Müllerbeisl, 1010, Seilerstätte 15 (512 42 65). Excellent cooking, pleasant surroundings. Open late.

Stadbeisl, 1010, Naglergasse 21 (533 33 23). Small, cozy and usually crowded at noon.

Smutny, 1010, Elisabethstr. 8 (587 13 56). A touch of old Vienna and the Third Man here. Excellent Budweiser beer, good food. Surroundings and waiters untouched by time and fashion. Open daily.

Tabakspfeife, 1010, Goldschmidg. 4 (63 72 86). Regular eating place for many Viennese. Wholesome good value. Closed Sat./Sun.

Tüv-Tam, 1020, Hollandstr. 3 (33 35 65). Strict orthodox Kosher cooking.

Weisse Rauchfangkehrer, 1010, Weihburgasse 4 (512 84 37). "The White Chimneysweep"—a series of rooms in Alpine *Stuben* style with hunting decor, strong on atmosphere. Austrian dishes and wines, with piano music after 8. Check the bill carefully before paying.

Zu Ebener Erd, 1070, Burggasse 13 (93 62 54). Lovely old Viennese house serving delicious local cuisine. DC, V. Closed Sun.

Zum Laterndl, 1010, Landesgerichtsstr. 12 (43 43 58). Near U.S. Library and University. Frequented by students. Good food. Closed Sat. and Sun.

Zur Lotte, 1190, Heiligenstädterstr. 179 (37 41 25). Excellent local cuisine, friendly atmosphere. Good wines and beers. Open daily.

Zur 10-er Marie, 1160, Ottakringerstr. 224 (46 31 16). Heuriger restaurant in an unexpected place. Genuine Schrammelmusik. Very romantic. Garden. Erstwhile haunt of Crown Prince Rudolph. Closed Sun., Mon.

Inexpensive
(see also *Wine Taverns* below)

Bierhof, 1010, Naglergasse 13 (533 44 28). Unusual beers and snacks. Open evenings till late, closed Mon.

Butterfass, 1020, Prater Hauptallee 122 (24 41 05). Near enough to be convenient, far enough from the Prater to afford peace. Simple Viennese food as the Viennese like it. Garden. Closed Mon. AE, DC, MC, V.

Reinthaler, 1010, Glückgasse 5 (512 33 66). Authentic gasthaus, neighborhood public included. Closed Fri. evening, Sat. and Sun.

Stadtkeller, 1010, Singerstr. 6 (512 12 69). Self service at bargain prices. Open daily from 10 A.M.

Schweizerhaus. In Prater (24 23 17) not far from the Big Wheel (from there, ask the way). Where the Viennese go to sit out and listen to the sounds of the funfair while consuming huge *Stelzen* (roast legs of pork), washed down with the best Budweiser in town.

Toni, 1010, Salzgries 6 (66 44 13). Specialty is grilled meats in Turkish and Yugoslav style. Open daily 8 A.M.–11 P.M.

Trzesniewski Buffet, 1010, Dorotheergasse 1 (512 32 91). Hidden away, just off Graben, with spicy canapés to eat on the spot or take away.

Zu den drei Hacken, 1010, Singerstr. (512 58 95). True Viennese *beisl* with simple, freshly-cooked food; large choice, excellent wines, lots of atmosphere, garden. Closed Sat. evenings and Sun.

Zum Braunen Hirschen, 1010, Rudolfsplatz 4 (533 64 62). Genuine Gasthaus, excellent value, friendly. Closed on weekends.

Excursion Dining

Fischerhaus (E), 1190, Hohenstr. (44 13 20). Reached only by car. Good view of the Wienerwald and parts of the city from outdoor terrace. Rustic furnishings. Expensive for what it is, but standards are high. Closed Mon. and 5 Nov. to 25 Feb. AE, DC, MC, V.

Tulbingerkogel Berghotel (E), A-3001, Tulbingerkogel (0 22 73 73 91). On the Tulbingerkogel hill in the Vienna Woods (30 minutes by car). Exceptional Viennese cuisine, Wachau white wines and Vöslau reds. There are also rooms, with bath. AE, DC, MC, V.

La Tour (E), Perchtoldsdorf, Hochstr. 17 (86 47 63). South of the city limits. One of the top luxury dining spots; beautiful setting, excellent food, glorious selection of cheeses and wines. Very expensive, but worth it. Closed Mon. AE, DC, MC, V.

Landhaus Winter (E), 1110, Simmeringerlände (76 23 17). On Danube Canal with summer terrace. Elegant; superb fish and other specialties. Delicious desserts. Children welcome. Closed Mon. AE, DC, MC, V.

Lusthaus (E), 1020, in Prater at end of the Hauptallee (74 17 87). First built in 1560 as the summer pavilion of Emperor Maximilian II. Rebuilt 1770 by Joseph II. Attractive cafe and restaurant. Open Thurs. to Tues. 9 A.M. to midnight.

Höldrichsmühle (M), A-2371, Hinterbrühl bei Mödling (02236–26274). Near Mödling, on the edge of Wienerwald, south of Vienna. Very fine fare from trout to *Milchrahmstrudel* (*strudel* with sour cream) at reasonable prices. Rooms.

Marchfelderhof (M), A-2232, Deutsch Wagram (02247–2243). 8 miles beyond the U.N. City, on the site of Napoleonic battle. Easily reached by *Schnellbahn* in half-an-hour from Wien Mitte station. 5 minutes' walk at the other end. The menu is immense and so are the portions, but prices are reasonable. Claustrophobia guaranteed. Reservations necessary, English spoken. Closed Mon. Rooms. AE, DC, MC, V.

Postschänke (M), 2392 Sulz/Wienerwald (02238/335). Very Biedermeier, typical Viennese excursion restaurant. You expect to see Franz Schubert at the next table. In the heart of the Vienna Woods; beautiful garden. Delicious, wholesome food.

WINE TAVERNS. These are mostly evening institutions intended primarily for drinking, but you can always get at least a bite and often a full dinner. They vary in class from simple to more ornate, and in originality from genuine to pseudo. One of their prominent features is the *Weinheber* (wine siphon), placed in front of you on the table. This should remind you that the wine was drawn straight out of the barrel. Nowadays, however, this is a strictly symbolic gesture since the wine is usually poured into the Weinheber straight from the bottle.

What will undoubtedly strike you as you enter your first wine cellar is the depth. Some of them are two or three floors down in the bowels of the earth and many of them consist of a network of cellars—merely a small part of the vast underground system that honeycombs its way below the streets of Vienna.

Some call themselves city Heurigers which, of course, is only for advertising purposes, since no authentic Heurigers can exist in the city. The Viennese call the more pretentious of these *Nobel-Heuriger,* defining them rather directly as being pretentious, probably overpriced, and less than genuine, although wines served are usually quite good.

Wine taverns in Vienna are many and even an old habitué can always discover a new one. Here are some of the better known ones.

Antiquitäten-Keller, 1060, Magdalenenstr. 32 (566 95 33). Open evenings 7–1; classical music. Closed Aug.

Augustinerkeller, 1010, Augustiner Str. 1 (533 10 26). Tucked in under the building which houses the great Albertina collection, and so handy for lunch (this one *is* open lunchtime) after sightseeing in the Hofburg. Simple and busy, but excellent value for money.

Esterhazykeller, 1010, Haarhof 1 (533 34 82). One of the most extensive—the deep cellars seem like an endless maze. Allow plenty of time on a busy night. Closes 9 P.M.

Melker Stiftskeller, 1010, Schottengasse 3 (533 55 30). Hidden at the back of a small courtyard, the entrance leads down and down, into one of the friendliest and most typical of all wine cellars. Excellent food and wine plus a hard-working clientele. Connected with Melk for a long way back. Evenings only. Closed Sun. and Aug.

Piaristenkeller, 1080, Piaristengasse 45 (42 91 52). Colorful, with restaurant service and zither music. Open late. Closed Mon. DC, MC.

Zwölf-Apostelkeller, 1010, Sonnenfelsgasse 3 (512 67 77). Not far from St. Stephen's. Frequented by students and deep below street level.

HEURIGERS. The *Heuriger* is a seasonal, very simply arranged wine tavern, attached to the premises of a vintner. There are around 700 families in Vienna growing wine, mostly in vineyards on the slopes of Kahlenburg and Bisamberg. Look for the certificate of authenticity on the door. It is here that you will find the best-known areas for wine—Nussdorf, Heiligenstadt, Grinzing, Sievering and Neustift. Other wine-growing regions are on the left bank of the Danube at Stammersdorf, Strebersdorf and Jedlersdorf, while the remoter Mauer and Oberlaa are to the south of the city. Heurigers in these latter districts are much less expensive and more authentic. The wine is sharp but pure and the food simple but good. Quiet courtyards to sit in more than make up for the effort in finding them.

Stammersdorf is especially recommended (Tram 31). Try **Robert Helm,** Stammersdorfer Str. 121 (39 12 44). The wine here will still be a *g'mischter Satz,* as it was in Schubert's day. This type of wine is produced from a variety of grapes, all grown in one vineyard and harvested and vinified together.

When the vintner has drawn off his new wine, he hangs a bough of pine over his door, inviting passers-by in to try his brew. The sale of wine in Vienna is strictly controlled and only the establishments that grow their vines entirely in Vienna or the surrounding rural districts can call themselves *heurigers.*

These delightful places sell food as well, usually local dishes, fairly basic and extremely tasty. You are served with wine by the waitresses—bumper glass mugs, *viertels* (each holding a ¼ liter)—but you have to collect the food yourself, buffet-style.

Naturally, summer and fall are the best time for visiting these outlying areas and spending a convivial evening. Almost all offer some form of mild entertainment, varying from an aged zither player to teams of folk singers extolling the glories of Vienna and its wine in a dialect so thick that not even visitors with fluent German can catch much of it. It's an institution of considerable charm and homely joy, the favorite Saturday afternoon or Sunday evening goal of thousands of Viennese. Here the entire family may go of an evening, bearing its own food or buying a plate of cold cuts and cheese at the wine house. It is all folksy and friendly, and in summer it is especially delightful, for then you sit in the patio or garden. Sadly, nowadays you might feel out of place taking your own food, so always inquire first.

A word of warning: Heurige wine tastes as mild as lemonade, but it is surprisingly potent and leaves a headache in its wake if it is of inferior quality. Austrians accustomed to the heurige eat almost constantly while drinking it, and many dilute it freely with soda water (*Gespritzt*). All good heurigers will furnish proof of the authenticity and purity of their wines on request.

A visit to these areas is possible in winter, too, though then it is the so-called *Noble-Heurigers* that come into their own. These are permanent wine taverns, with classic interiors, often warmed by attractive tiled stoves—like survivals from rich peasant houses.

The easiest to get to (if you don't have a car), are located in Grinzing, Sievering and Nussdorf, which can be reached with streetcar 38, bus 39A and streetcar D respectively. The Vienna Tourist Board puts out an excellent little booklet which will tell you all you want to know about *heuriger* as well as listing many of the best ones; it is called, naturally enough, *Heuriger in Wien* and gives addresses, opening dates and directions on how to reach that district. Our favorite is Stammersdorf, but almost equally high on the list are **Martin Sepp,** Coblenzlgasse 34 in Grinzing (32 32 33); **Haslinger,** 1190, Agnesgasse 3 in Sievering (44 13 47); **Schübl-Auer,** 1190, Kahlenbergerstr. 22 in Nussdorf (37 22 22); and **Stift Schotten,** 1190, Hackhofergasse 17, also in Nussdorf (37 15 75).

CAFES. The old-fashioned Viennese type of cafe, with its marble tables, newspapers, sidewalk terraces in warm weather, is an institution of long tradition that has strengthened its position here and there by adding buffets or partial restaurant service and espresso machines. All of the Viennese cafes offer pastries.

Here we can mention only a few of Vienna's 15,000-odd cafes, ranging from small espresso bars to venerable club-like institutions on and inside the Ring.

Except for those belonging to the famous hotels, mentioned previously, some of the most typical old-fashioned cafes in Vienna are—**Alte Backstube**, 1080, Lange Gasse 34, beautiful Baroque house, lovingly furnished, excellent pastries, open late; **Raimund,** where men of letters meet, at Volksgartenstr. 5, across from the Volkstheater; **Bräunerhof,** 1010, Stallburgg. 2, with music at weekends; **Mozart,** with very pleasant summer lunches on the street terrace, at Albertinaplatz 2, near the Opera; **Prückel** with restaurant service, Stubenring 24, across the street from the Stadtpark; **Tirolerhof,** Fuhrichgasse 8, across the square from Albertina, sometimes afternoon music; **Cafe Central,** 1010, Freyung/Herrengasse in Ferstelpalais complex, a piece of history brought back to life, where Stalin and Trotsky used to play chess; beautiful. Closed in winter; the 100-years-old **Schwarzenberg** on the Ring corner at Schwarzenberg Square; **Frauenhuber,** Himmelpfortgasse 6, all with restaurant service; **Ritter,** Mariahilferstr. 73; **Haag,** at Schottengasse 2, with a garden; **Museum,** corner of Friedrichstr.–Operngasse; **Sperl,** 1060, Gumpendorferstr. 11, a landmark, one of the most famous of all, newly restored.

Cafe Laudon, 1080, Laudongasse 24, a cafe-restaurant with tradition, popular with the chess set. AE.

Among the better modern cafes is **Cafe Europa,** on the ground floor of the hotel of the same name, with large windows facing the Kärntnerstrasse.

The most important downtown coffeehouses are **Cafe Hawelka,** 1010, Dorotheergasse, just off Graben, a meeting place for artists, always crowded. Open 7 A.M. to 2 A.M. except Tues., Sun. 4 P.M. to 2 A.M.; **Cafe Sacher,** behind the Opera House, famous for its cake and its elegance; and **Cafe Landtman,** 1010, on Schottenring, AE, which is a distinguished meeting place for civil servants through its location near the Rathaus, Parliament and headquarters of leading political parties.

Cafes with music—**Kursalon** (also restaurant) in the City Park (Stadtpark), large and popular outdoor cafe during the warmer months with a band playing Austrian light music in the late afternoon and evening. AE. **Volksgarten,** afternoon and evening, with dancing.

PASTRY SHOPS. Demel, the famous pastry shop at 1010, Kohlmarkt 14 (533 55 16), offers at lunch time also magnificent snacks of delicate meats, fish and vegetables. Try stuffed mushrooms or vegetable-cheese combinations. Gorgeous coffee and hot chocolate. Filling your stomach will mean emptying your pocketbook. Open daily 10–6. AE, MC.

Other top pastry shops include: **Gerstner,** Kärntnerstr. 15 (512 49 63); **Heiner,** Kärntnerstr. 21 (512 68 63), with a nice upstairs room, and at Wollzeile 9 (512 48 38); **Lehmann,** Graben 12 (512 18 15). The ubiquitous but less scrumptious **Aida** chain is in the Inner City at Opern Ring 7, Stock-im-Eisenplatz 2, near St. Stephen's and at Wollzeile 28—excellent coffee and pastries at low prices.

Another favorite is **Sluka,** 1010, Rathausplatz 8 (43 88 96). Pretty shop with some of the best pastries and cakes in Vienna. Highly recommended.

The **Kurkonditorei** in Kurhaus Oberlaa, 1100 (68 16 11), is superb and worth a visit. Afterwards there is a park with a naturally-heated swimming pool in which you can work off the calories. You could then call in at the

Reumannplatz and have one of the best ice creams in the world at **Salon Tichy**. There is another swimming pool on the Reumannplatz. The Amalienbad is an indoor complex built in 1926 and now restored to its Art Decor splendor. If you haven't time to travel so far, visit the "Stadthaus" of the Kurkonditorei on the Neuer Markt 16 (513 29 36), and then swing over to Hoher Markt 4 for a breathtaking ice cream at Eissalon Garda.

SPORTS. It is perhaps a surprise to discover that Vienna, a center of arts and sciences of long tradition, is also extremely active in sports. The probable explanation is the average Austrian's love for nature and outdoors. Vienna possesses over 100 sports fields and about 400 recreation grounds, not even counting the two main establishments which are the large **Stadium** in Prater (about 90,000 spectators) and the unique **Stadthalle** (city convention and recreation hall) on Vogelweidplatz near Westbahnhof (17,000 spectators).

BICYCLING. All over Austria tracks are being set up. Bikes can be hired from: 1020, Vivariumstr. 8 (26 66 44); 1020, Praterstern Station (26 85 57); 1100, Waldg. (64 10 113); 1190, Heiligenstädterstr. 180 at DDSG landing, Nussdorf. (37 45 98); or most conveniently, Franz Josefs-Kai, by the Salztorbrücke, on the Danube canal.

GOLF. For golf, you also have to head out to Prater. *Golf-Club Wien* is located at Freudenaustrasse 65a (74 17 86), at the end of the Prater Hauptallee. The course is open from April to Dec.; 18 holes, total length (out and home) 5,810 meters, which is about 6,020 yards. The clubhouse has a restaurant, closed Mon. Guests are welcome. Fees on weekends and holidays are a little higher. The other club is at Wiener Neustadt, the *Föhrenwald-Wiener Neustadt,* (02622/52 171), also with 18 holes, open April–Dec.

HIKING AND CLIMBING. The Austrian national summer sports are hiking and mountain climbing and the Viennese love doing both. Wienerwald—which can be reached by several streetcars and buses—offers any number of walks, light and hard, as short as half an hour and as long as the 220-km. (137-mile) path to Mödling. Pathways are well marked.

The nearest place for rock climbing is Hohe Wand (primarily for training) but the Styrian Alps are only a few hours' drive from the city. Consult the *Österreichischer Alpenverein* which has several branches in Vienna, including Rotenturmstr. 14 (513 10 03) and Walfischgasse 12 (512 69 33).

HORSERACING AND RIDING. For turf fans, there are spring, summer, and fall events at the two racetracks in Prater; flat-racing at Freudenau (74 16 09) and trotting at Krieau (57 72 58).

Horses for riding are available at various riding schools such as *Wiener Reitclub,* Barmherzigengasse 17, 3rd District, *Reitverein St. Stephan,* Weingartenalle, 22nd District, and *Reitschule Kottas,* in Freudenau.

TENNIS. There are many openair tennis courts. Larger ones are in Prater, in the Eislaufverein in Heumarkt (in summer), in Pötzleinsdorf and Hietzing. There are several tennis schools, among them those at Döblinger Hauptstr. 48, 19th District, at Bergmüllergasse 8, 14th District, and in the suburb of Mauer, Kaserngasse 3, which also has indoor courts. Any problem finding somewhere to play, just ask your hotel concierge.

WATER SPORTS. Rowing. The Danube offers many possibilities for rowing. There are about 20 sets of boathouses and numerous rowing clubs. Boats can be rented near the Wagramerstrasse bridge on the left bank of the Old Danube. For further information inquire at the *Österreichischer Ruderverband,* Austrian Rowing Association, 1040, Prinz Eugen-Str. 12 (505 73 07).

Sailing. Sailing boats can be rented on the Old Danube, where there is also a sailing school. *Union-Yacht Club* and *Wiener Yacht-Club* have their boathouses here. The *Vienna Festival Regatta* takes place each June during the Vienna Festival and the Vienna Championship in the fall. Sailing information from *Haus des Sports,* 1040, Prinz Eugen-Str. 12 (505 37 42).

Swimming. There are many openair swimming pools and several bathing establishments on the Danube. One of the best in the open is the *Stadium* pool in Prater, and the most popular among the Danube bathing establishments is Gänsehäufel Island near Kaisermühlen on the Old Danube (cross Reichsbrücke and turn right).

Donau Insel (the Danube Island) is a large recreation area on an artificial island. Its beach, several miles long, runs from Florisdorf well into the Lobau region. You can get there by car (to Florisdorfer Brücke, Reichsbrücke or Praterbrücke, or by U1 as far as Donau Insel).

But perhaps the prettiest is the Krapfenwald pool in Grinzing, near the Cobenzl and overlooking the city. Take the 38 streetcar to Grinzing, then bus 38S.

The best among the indoor establishments are the Stadthallenbad next to Stadthalle and the Dianabad complex just across the canal, which replaces the old turn-of-the-century Dianabad, which in turn replaced the site where *The Blue Danube* was first performed.

WINTER SPORTS. The Austrian national winter sport is **skiing,** but in Vienna the snow usually does not stay long at a time. With sufficient snow, there is very good skiing in various sections of Wienerwald, especially on the Hohe Wand Wiese slope, which is within the city limits (in the 14th District), and which even boasts a 400-meter-long ski lift; in case there is not enough snow, the ten so-called "snow guns" present here produce it artificially. There is also "grass-skiing" here in summer.

On Donau Insel (Danube Island) there is a new cross-country skiing trail accessible from Florisdorfer Brücke.

Otherwise the Vienna skiing grounds are on Semmering, Schneeberg, Hochkar, Türnitz, Annaberg, Josephsberg, and Raxalpe, about 2 slow driving or riding hours from the city, and in Mariazell which is a little farther.

Ice skating is also very popular in Vienna. There are more than 50 ice skating rinks, among them some artificial ones. The artificial openair skating rink of **Eislaufverein** (Ice Skating Union) is at Heumarkt 2 between the Konzerthaus and the Intercontinental Hotel. You can rent skates for a small fee.

EATING THE AUSTRIAN WAY

Schlagobers Supreme

In the course of centuries, Slavs, Turks, Italians, Magyars and, of course, Germans, all flourished within the immediate homeland of the Habsburgs. It might be reasonable to suppose that Austria, the inheritor of the remnants of the Empire, would have a cuisine composed of all these varied and exotic elements, fused into one great big cosmopolitan gastronomic United Nations. But it doesn't work out like that. It is true that you will encounter Hungarian restaurants, Balkan restaurants, Italian restaurants, even Russian restaurants in Vienna and other important cities of Austria, but during their long residence in Austria, the various exotic schools of cooking have become Austrianized. Asperities have been smoothed away, exaggerations toned down, and the gamut of tastes brought into harmony. But the chief contribution of the people who created the Viennese waltz and the operetta naturally comes with the dessert course, in the appropriate form of rich and luscious pastries, and in the beloved and universal *Schlagobers* or whipped cream.

This means that the visitor to Austria, while he will be able to enjoy a wide range of international dishes, need not fear that his palate or his stomach will be attacked by fiery or pungent concoctions. He will be able to order without fear anything he discovers on the menu. He will certainly find it advisable to watch his weight, however, because Austrian food is filling, rich, and copious. The portions may strike visitors from countries of less hearty eaters as enormous. But if the new arrival, eating his first meal, is under the impression that he is being so well served because he has stumbled on the one substantial repast of the day, with perhaps a little

81

minor help on a couple of other occasions, he will be quite wrong. Austrians not only eat a lot at one time, they eat a good many times during the day.

Pastry Shops

In case of a feeling of faintness between meals (and in case any time is being wasted between meals), one can always dart into one of the *Konditorei* or pastry shops so numerous in Austria, or the milk and *espresso* bars, now fairly widespread, for a life-preserving snack. The pastry shop *is* thoroughly Austrian. Other countries have pastry shops, but they aren't the same and they don't play so important a role in the daily life of the citizen. A visit to a famous pastry shop, like Demel's on the Kohlmarkt in Vienna, or Zauner's in Bad Ischl, is a must. Both of these shops achieved their fame as imperial court caterers and so far have succeeded in preserving their quality in spite of contemporary difficulties in finding the staff to carry on the pastrycook's delicate art. Many pastry shops do not confine their temptations to pastries alone. They also offer sandwiches, vegetable soufflés, mushrooms stuffed with a herb and cheese mixture, in fact all manner of heavenly tidbits.

All-Purpose Coffeehouses

To savor the atmosphere of the coffeehouses you must take your time. In Vienna you have a wide choice of these establishments; set aside an afternoon, a morning, or at least a couple of hours, and settle down in one of your choice. You can read (many coffeehouses carry not only Austrian papers and magazines but a few English or American ones) or you can catch up on letter writing. There is no need to worry about outstaying one's welcome, even over a single small cup of Mokka.

The decline of the coffeehouse has fortunately been halted, and even reversed. They represent a way of life that is once more sought-after: many coffeehouses are being refurbished and new ones are opening.

The Austrian coffeehouse has a lengthy history. When the Turkish invaders were driven out of Vienna in 1683 they left behind some mysterious brown beans. A former Austrian spy in the Turkish camp learned how to use them. Thus coffee was introduced to Austria, and the first coffeehouse established. This was a momentous moment, for a substantial part of Austrian social life revolves around the coffeehouses. They are scattered all over the nation. They are the club, pub and bistro all rolled into one. They are the places where one meets business associates, relaxes over the paper and generally finds a home from home.

Coffee is not just coffee in Austria. It comes in many forms and under many names. Morning coffee is generally *Melange* (half coffee and half milk), or with little milk, a *Brauner*. The usual afterdinner drink is *Mokka,* very black, and most Austrians like it heavily sweetened. But that is just the beginning. Some restaurants, notably those specializing in Balkan cookery, serve Turkish coffee (*Türkischer*), a strong, thick brew. There is usually considerable sediment in the bottom of the cup, which should not be stirred, and the coffee is often served with a square of Turkish Delight.

More delightful to Western eyes are the coffee-and-whipped-cream combinations (*Kaffee mit Schlag*), but these are tastes that are easily acquired and a menace to all but the very thin. The coffee may be either hot or cold. A customer who wants more whipped cream than coffee asks for a *Doppelschlag.* Hot black coffee in a glass with one knob of whipped cream is an *Einspänner* (one-horse coach). Then you can go to town on a *Mazagran,* black coffee with ice and a tot of rum, or *Eiskaffee,* cold coffee with ice cream, whipped cream and biscuits. Or you can simply order a *Portion Kaffee* and have an honest pot of coffee and jug of hot milk. As you can see, coffee-drinking is a life's work.

The Restaurant Scene

As in any large cosmopolitan community, you can dine in Vienna in an atmosphere of luxury with perfect service and delicious food, including not only the best of Austrian cooking but beautifully prepared foods from other lands. In Vienna, you can also find a tasty meal for a comparatively modest sum. In the larger cities, such as Graz and Innsbruck, there is a similar selection of eating places, although on a smaller scale and with lower prices generally. Out in the country—except in the fashionable tourist resorts—you may enjoy good, modest meals at still lower prices.

The one thing that is common to restaurants throughout the country, whether they are pricey Viennese ones or simple country inns, is that they have a great deal of character, friendliness and atmosphere. This is partly due to the fact that the Austrians have preserved a lot of ceremony and the niceties of social etiquette in their lives, with the result that the rate of change has been much slower in Austria than in many other parts of Europe. But something of a revolution has been taking place in Vienna and to a lesser extent outside. Many new restaurants are opening and new ways of presenting old dishes have been developed with varying success. Emphasis has been placed on local dishes. The Austrian National Tourist Office encouraged restaurants to offer traditional meals, characteristic of their region, and they responded enthusiastically. But, to repeat a point made elsewhere, these local dishes were originally cooked on farms for hard-working hands who needed both sustenance and bulk in their diet—so they tend to be both hearty and rich. You might want to have a schnapps afterwards to help the digestion!

Consult the restaurant guides (first and foremost *Gault Millau Österreich,* if you can cope with German) and restaurant columns in the daily papers.

Don't leave paying the bill till the last minute; Austrian headwaiters are never in a hurry to collect your money. It is customary to add a tip of up to 10% to the final total.

Austrian Specialties

One of the best food buys in Austria is soup, which is consistently good—and inexpensive. Austrian soups range all the way from the highly seasoned *Gulyassuppe,* full of paprika and onions, to mild consommé with a poached egg. Particularly popular with Austrians and visitors is the *Leberknödlsuppe,* a meat broth containing liver dumplings. It contains less calories for the weight-conscious than the many other delicious noodle soups.

Having no seacoast, Austria is naturally not fish country, except for the freshwater varieties. Carp, Fogosch, pike and, best of all, succulent crawfish (when in season, which is rather short) and various trout from the native lakes and rivers are the best bet. Carp is an insipid-tasting fish to those used to the lively savor of the deep sea. Pike and Fogosch come from the Danube and the lakes on the Hungarian border and are often excellent when grilled or fried, much like pike and bass. The crawfish (called Krebs) look like tiny lobsters and make a delicious thick soup in many restaurants. Or they are served cold to be laboriously picked from their shells and dipped in mayonnaise.

Austrian brook trout and rainbow trout are delicious. The most popular way of serving them is "blue," the whole fish boiled in a *court bouillon* and accompanied by drawn butter. Or try it *Müllerin*—sautéed in butter to a crisp brown. In summer try cold smoked trout for a delicate entrée.

If you happen to be in Austria on Ash Wednesday, don't miss a *Hering-schmaus*. On this the strictest fast-day in the church calendar, the Austrians adhere to it by eating no meat. Instead, just about every restaurant holds the above-named feast—a buffet packed with every fish and salad specialty imaginable.

Schnitzels and Other Meat Dishes

Veal and beef dominate the Austrian kitchen, though the various types of schnitzel can also be pork. *Wiener Schnitzel* is usually veal steak, well beaten, dipped in flour, egg and crumbs and fried, usually in deep fat, to golden brown crunchiness. *Natur Schnitzel* is fried as it is, without egg or crumbs. *Holstein Schnitzel* is the same, plus a fried egg on the meat and crossed anchovy strips on the egg. *Pariser Schnitzel* is dipped in flour and egg and fried. There are many other types of schnitzel and related veal specialties. One of the best is *Cordon Bleu:* cheese and ham are rolled in a piece of veal, the whole is dipped as above and fried. *Paprikaschnitzel* is also good.

Pork is highly popular and also less expensive than veal. There's plain roast pork with potatoes or *Knödeln* (dumplings like doughy cannonballs); special cuts like *Schweinscarré*, or a long tender strip from beside the backbone called *Schweinsjungfrau* ("pig's virgin," if you must be literal), and such specialties as pig's shank, kidneys, and a great variety of smoked pork dishes.

Austrians don't care much for lamb, but it is now more widely available than a few years ago. However, venison (*Rehrücken*) and numerous other game dishes (wild boar, hare, pheasant, quail, partridge) are popular and usually served with cranberries. Some of these game dishes are of considerable antiquity, even medieval, and have vanished from the tables of most Western countries.

Steaks are usually good in Austria. Note that the odd word *Lungenbraten* may be used to denote what is also called *Filet.* Ask for your steak *durch* (well done), *medium* (medium rare) or *Englisch* (rare).

Austrian *Tafelspitz* (boiled beef) is famous, and deservedly so. It is prepared by being put into boiling water and simmered for about two hours, until it is well cooked. With it come various sauces, a bland sauce, like a thin hollandaise, flavored with chives; and more tangy sauces of grated horseradish, or horseradish and apple which are combined raw and allowed to fuse into a delicious form of dynamite. *Röstkartoffeln* (roasted sliced potatoes) are usually served with the beef, and sometimes a number of other vegetables.

At the other end of the taste gamut is *Gulyas* (goulash), of Hungarian origin, made with beef—or best of all, venison. Highly seasoned, it is usually served with potatoes. Reminiscent of the New England boiled dinner is *Bauernschmaus,* a tasty meat dish of the folksy type. It varies from restaurant to restaurant but usually includes ham, a piece of salt pork, sausage, sauerkraut, and a large dumpling.

Sausage and Chicken

Austrian sausages are excellent. If you want to try a sampling of a number of different varieties, you can order a sausage platter, and you will be given a generous selection of cold sliced sausages. Frankfurters, named after a Viennese butcher, are excellent and are called *Wieners* almost everywhere—*except* in Vienna.

Austrian cuisine offers two superb chicken dishes: *Backhuhn* or *Backhendl,* young, medium-sized chicken breaded and fried in deep fat until it is golden brown; and *Steirisches Brathuhn,* roast chicken, usually turned on a spit. Vienna is believed to be the home territory of the Backhendl, while Styria, where the best chickens in Austria are raised, is the home of the Brathuhn, also called *Poulard.*

The Knödl is an Austrian institution. It leads both rice and potatoes in popularity, but not by much. There is an infinite variety of this dough dish. One group includes the homely hearty unsweetened type, the dumpling, which appears with meat or goes into soup. Then there are the smaller, more delicate sweet ones, eaten as dessert, flavored with jam, poppy seed, cottage cheese, and other unusual ingredients.

There are also fine cheeses, the best of which is the Vorarlberg Farmhouse *Bergkäse* from the villages of the Bregenzerwald.

Vegetables and Bread

Although Austria is not famous for vegetable cookery, it has several delightful specialties. Puréed spinach (*Spinat*) is cooked spinach, chopped and flavored with butter, salt, garlic, perhaps a bit of flour, and a little cream. *Rotkraut* (red cabbage), made sweet-sour and flavored with caraway seed is also good. Mushrooms, fried to a delicious crispness in the manner of Wiener Schnitzel, are not uncommon in better restaurants. Stuffed green peppers and stuffed cabbage in tomato sauce are contributions of Hungarian and Balkan cooking to the Austrian menu.

A fairly good green salad, generally lettuce with a vinegar and oil dressing, usually somewhat sweetened, is served almost anywhere. If you don't like sugar in your salad dressing, say so when you order. A popular alternative, which may or may not please English and American palates, is a *Gemischter Salat,* a dab of several cooked and raw vegetables—not mixed greens as in the States and England; these dabs are neatly arranged in a ring on a plate—a bit of kraut, chopped beets, shredded lettuce, etc. *Slaw,* or cabbage salad, is popular, with a vinegar dressing.

Bread is crisp and excellent, perhaps the best in the world. It will pay any visitor making a long stay to go to a *Bäckerei* (bakery), sample some of the fine breads, and see which ones suit their particular taste. Incidentally, bread and sweet cakes or pastries are not generally made in the same bakery, as they are in the States or in England. You buy fine *Torten,* which are extremely rich cakes, only in pastry shops, never in bakeries. Also, let no unwary visitor look at his pocket dictionary and order *Kuchen,* expecting to receive a beautiful piece of iced, many-layered cake. What he will probably get is a sort of coffee cake or sweet roll, which often turns up as dessert in Austria.

Semmels and salt sticks and the like are commonly served with meals, along with dark rye bread of various types. Wholemeal bread is to be found in every bakery.

Cheese

After years in the doldrums, the Austrian cheese industry has accepted the challenge posed by massive imports, and a wide variety of all sorts of cheeses, carefully made in small quantities, is beginning to come onto the market. Most famous is the Vorarlberg mountain cheese made from raw milk fresh from the Alm. It's a must for cheese lovers.

All About Desserts

And now the desserts—those fabulous desserts! It is impossible to choose the best, for there are so many wonderful sweets, but perhaps the best known is *Strudel.* There are many kinds of strudel, most of them made with fruit, a few with cheese. There are apple strudel, cottage cheese strudel, cherry strudel, strudel made with fruit and nuts, strudel made with fruit and nuts and raisins—and a most delicious Pannonian variety with apples, raisins and poppy seeds, available only in Burgenland.

Palatschinken, thin dessert pancakes, are a distant relative of the French crêpes. They are rolled around a stuffing of fruit, jam, nuts, or other delicious tidbits. *Salzburger Nockerl* is one of the most famous Austrian desserts. It is a delicious soufflé of eggs, sugar, butter, and a bit of flour. Pick your restaurant carefully for this tasty item and don't hurry the chef. It's worth waiting for.

Kaiserschmarren, meaning imperial fluff, is a thicker pancake than the Palatschinken at the beginning of its preparation, but as it is shredded during the cooking process before it becomes quite firm, and is dusted with sugar and served with stewed fruit (mainly plums called *Zwetschkenröster*), it doesn't look anything like a pancake.

Torte is an Austrian specialty and may be very good or very poor. The most famous is the *Sachertorte,* created at the Sacher Hotel in Vienna nearly a hundred years ago. It is a very rich chocolate cake iced with more chocolate. Compare *Sachertorte* from the Sacher Hotel, with apricot jam in the middle, with *Sacher Torte* from Demel's; they put the apricot jam just below the icing! The use of this renowned name was the subject of a much-publicized trial, which came to a decision worthy of Solomon, that the original article should be spelled as one word, those others using the similar recipe must use two words.

Other names in the Torte world are *Dobosch,* hazelnut, *Linzer, Malakoff.* If these rich desserts are too much for the visitor, he may want to try *Guglhupf,* a fine-textured sponge cake, good with coffee. A popular specialty is the *Krapfen,* which used to turn up during Fasching (the Carnival season) and is now available all year. It is a relative of the jam-filled doughnut of Britain, but better, because it is fluffier and crisper.

Characteristic Viennese confections are *Marillenknödel* and *Zwetschkenknödel* made from apricots and plums from which the stones are removed and replaced by lumps of sugar, after which the fruit is wrapped in a light potato-flour dough and boiled before being rolled in buttered breadcrumbs. Then there are the yeast dumplings filled with plum jam (*Powidl*) rolled in poppy seeds and sugar—order just one, the size may surprise you. And *Powidltatschkerl* (more difficult to pronounce than to eat), thin potato dough triangles enclosing again plum jam, this time rolled in breadcrumbs with hot butter and sugar.

A Small Glossary of Specifically Austrian Food Terms:

Ananas	can mean strawberries as well as pineapple
Erdäpfel	potatoes
Faschiertes	minced meat
Fisolen	green beans
Karfiol	cauliflower
Kohlsprossen	brussels sprouts
Marille	apricot
Paradeiser	tomatoes
Schlagobers	whipped cream
Stelze	leg of pork

AUSTRIA'S WINES

Treading the Wine Road

by
NICHOLAS ALLEN

Nicholas Allen is an Englishman, resident in Vienna for more than 20 years, who heads a scheme that takes English-language plays (Thornton Wilder's among them) to schools throughout the country. He knows the highways and byways—especially the byways—of Austria as only someone who spends every winter struggling with avalanches and village inns can.

The cultivation of grapes and the making of wine can be traced in Austria back to Celtic times, even before the Romans arrived. Despite many setbacks over the long centuries winemaking has continued to be a major industry right up to the present day with 250,000 people at work in some 50,000 wineries to produce an average of 3 million hectoliters of wine a year.

Vines have the tendency to thrive in beautiful surroundings and, as attractive buildings and towns often develop close to vineyards, a journey through any wine region can be an alluring prospect. Luckily, Austria has been largely neglected by the "experts," and its deliciously fresh wines will form an ideal treasure-trove to reward those who enjoy drinking wine and dislike the all-too-frequent nonsense that goes with it. One of the things that can impede the easy enjoyment of wine and its creation is the aura of mystique which so often surrounds it, the do's and don't's which have more to do with snobbery than with a love of wine.

This chapter describes a journey that loops through Austria's wine country, one that will give you plenty of chance to sample the changing landscape as well as the varieties of wine. Many of the towns you will pass through are mentioned in other chapters, so the concentration here is on the wine itself. But before starting out, it is worth relaying some basic information about Austrian wine, to provide a background.

Starting with the Romans

Not long after the Roman emperor Domitian had banned the making of wine outside Italy (around 90 A.D.)—an edict that proved hard to enforce—another emperor, Probus, took the more sensible line of encouraging winemaking throughout the empire. He did so particularly in Austria, where the Danube vineyards date back to his time.

Another emperor—Charlemagne—of what had, by then, become the Holy Roman Empire, ordered the bishoprics and monasteries in his lands to oversee the making of wine, thus ensuring continuity through difficult times. To this day there are many monasteries involved in the making of wine in Austria.

Winemaking wasn't easy in those early days. In 1456 the vintage was so sour that the emperor of the time ordered it to be poured into the rivers. In Vienna, however, he decreed that the undrinkable crop be used to mix the mortar for the tower of St. Stephen's Cathedral. It is a miracle that the finished result is not like the Tower of Pisa.

Governments have always been in need of money and they quickly realized that wine was a good source of tax income. During the 16th century the Bavarians evaded these taxes by making—and drinking—more and more beer instead of wine. The Austrians, however, remained faithful to wine and have done so to the present day.

The 19th century spelled disaster everywhere. Phylloxera killed the vines throughout Europe and it took well into the 20th century before new, resistant vines were established and bearing in their place. Then came World War I which left Austria an amputated shadow of its former self. Half its vineyards disappeared behind new boundaries and were lost to other countries forever.

During the 1920s the economic stability of Austria's wine industry was ensured by the development of the *Hochkultur*. Professor Lenz Moser from Krems had the idea of training vines on stakes and letting them leaf and flower at a height of 3–4 feet; this made cultivation, protection, and harvesting much easier and also increased the yield.

During Hitler's Third Reich Austrian wine was submerged into the German wine industry, so it was not until 1955—with the signing of the State Treaty—that the Austrian wine industry was ready to begin the upward course which has continued to the present day.

The "anti-freeze" scandals of 1985 were a big setback for the Austrian wine industry. However, the nation has risen to the occasion, introducing some of the strictest legislation in the world to ensure that such things won't happen again. It is worth pointing out that not one winery on our journey, and not one wine mentioned in this chapter, has been even remotely involved, and that even at the height of the scandal at least 95% of Austrian wines were blameless. By 1988 the beneficial effects of these measures had become apparent. Austrian wines are better than ever before and represent good value for high quality and great variety. Rebuilding its international image will be a long process, but an impressive start has been made by the Austrian wine industry.

A Red and White Dossier

Austrian wines are fresh and usually drunk young. Economics and local preference have led people to underestimate these wines' ability to age and mature. Austrian winemakers tend to let their wines ferment through until there is little residual sugar left; this makes them very different from their sweeter German cousins.

Until recently only the white wines have been of any interest, but in the last ten years there has been a major development leading to some red wines of quality. Winemakers in Austria face the opposite problem to that of their Californian colleagues: in California the steady hot climate leads to magnificent red wines and whites that can easily be too full and heavy, while in Austria the raw climate leads to crisp, clean white wines but to reds that often lack body and roundness. Over recent years there has been a marked trend towards maturing red wines in small oak barrels (*barriques*), thus producing wines with a higher tannin content and more body. These wines take longer to mature but the results are already proving to be wines that are far more complex and interesting.

Here is a list of the seven "types" of wine you may encounter on the wine-road trip:

Tafel- or *Land-wein*—table wine, of Austrian grapes, usually served open and good to "quaff."
Qualitätswein—wine of a specific region and grape conforming to certain standards. Quality wine must be "harmonious" and "typical."
Kabinett—quality wine with no sugar added during fermentation.
Spätlese—late-gathered grapes give rise to a rich, powerful wine which, unlike its German equivalent, need not be sweet.
Auslese—a wine made from late-gathered grapes that have been individually sorted for quality before being crushed.
Beerenauslese—grapes that have been left on the vine to become raisin-like. Attacked by *noble-rot* these grapes are then made into magnificent dessert wines equal to the great Sauternes.
Eiswein—grapes picked when frozen by December frosts. This specialty, found in the Burgenland, is savored drop by drop.

These are the principal grapes found in Austrian wine:

White: *Grüner Veltliner*—a sturdy wine which accounts for 30% of vines in Austria. Particularly at home in lower Austria it can, if cultivated for quality rather than quantity produce great white wines. They are dry, with touch of fruit, fresh to the taste often with a "peppery" aftertaste. This grape is unique to Austria.
Müller Thurgau—a Riesling Sylvaner cross that produces mild rather uninteresting wines.
Welschriesling—found in Burgenland and Styria this grape gives wines of great elegance when allowed to be really dry.
Pinot blanc—the French White Burgundy grape is being planted extensively with good results. When not too heavy the wines have exceptional

aroma. Several growers are experimenting with the Chardonnay grape, noble cousin to pinot blanc.

Neuburger—legend has it that in 1860 two growers found this vine floating down the Danube as driftwood. They planted it near Dürnstein and ever since it has produced beautiful wines of a nutty quality; some are dry, some less so.

Rheinriesling—as in Germany, this noblest of all white wine grapes produces superb, dry white wines that mature for many years. At its best in the Wachau.

Muscat Ottonel—a difficult vine that produces delightful muscat-flavoured wines. They range from dry in the Wachau to sweet in the Burgenland.

Zierfandler and Rotgipfler—the two grapes at the heart of the world-famous Gumpoldskirchner wines. Rich, heady and lasting.

Red: *Blauer Portugieser*—when not used for mass wines these can be distinguished. At its best round Retz.

Blaufränkisch—introduced from Franconia at the time of Charlemagne, this is the grape of the Burgenland where many of Austria's finest red wines are produced. At their best these are full, dry and with enough tang to make them interesting.

Blauburgunder—the Pinot Noir from Burgundy also produces good wines but the climate makes it impossible for them ever to come close to the French cousins.

Zweigelt and St. Laurent—two specifically Austrian cross-breeds that can occasionally produce surprising results.

Blauer Wildbacher—a grape unique for hundreds of years to a small corner of West Styria. It produces the wine called *Schilcher*.

These two lists form the basis of the great variety which is Austrian wine; it is hardly known outside the country because both wineries and their output are usually too small to make export and wide marketing viable propositions. This makes it all the more exciting to set off on a journey of discovery.

The journey I am going to suggest is a personal one; it leaves many gaps along the way for the traveler to discover for himself. After all, what is more fun than that wine you—and only you—have unearthed from a small grower in a tiny village—. But before launching on the journey, here are a couple of points to bear in mind.

Always ask on the spot about the vintage: in a climate as varied and as unstable as Austria's there can be great regional differences from year to year. Wine lists in restaurants are now much more informative and extensive, and wine waiters will usually be eager to help you.

Stop wherever you feel interested: no matter whether it is a vineyard or a cellar, a private house or a co-operative, a gasthaus or the smartest restaurant. Those involved, be they in the Seewinkel or in Dürnstein will be pleased to show you around, talk to you, let you taste their wines and maybe at the end of it all even sell you the odd bottle that will surprise your friends back home.

The Wine Trail Begins

The journey starts in Spitz an oder Donau. You could take the West-autobahn from Vienna as far as Melk and, after looking at the famous

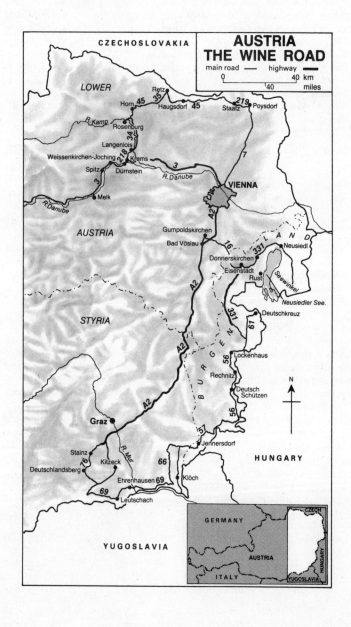

CZECHOSLOVAKIA

AUSTRIA
THE WINE ROAD
main road — highway ━━
0   40   km
       40   miles

LOWER

Retz
Horn   45   35
     Haugsdorf   45   Staatz   219   Poysdorf
R. Kamp
Rosenburg
34
Langenlois
Weissenkirchen-Joching   218   Krems   3
Spitz   Dürnstein
3   R. Danube
7
Melk
R. Danube   VIENNA
A21

AUSTRIA

Gumpoldskirchen
Bad Vöslau   L A N D
16   331   Neusiedl
Donnerskirchen
Eisenstadt
Rust   Seewinkel
Neusiedler See.

STYRIA

331
191   Deutschkreuz

A2
56   Lockenhaus
Rechnitz
Deutsch
Schützen
N

A2   56

57
Graz   Jennersdorf
HUNGARY
Stainz
R. Mur   66
76   Kitzeck
Deutschlandsberg   69
Ehrenhausen   69   Klöch
69   Leutschach

YUGOSLAVIA

GERMANY   CZECH
AUSTRIA
ITALY   HUNGARY
YUGOSLAVIA

BURGENLAND

monastery, cross the Danube by the magnificent new bridge. On the other side you join Route 3 and drive 16 km. (10 miles) downstream to Spitz. Villages with ancient churches nestle against the slopes and where there aren't vines there are apricot trees. A drive along this road at blossom-time (usually late April) is unforgettable. Come back in August and eat your fill of golden apricots bought at the roadside.

The vineyards begin at Spitz. Here the Danube valley is high and narrow, reminiscent of the Rhine. The wise Roman Emperor Probus ordered his soldiers to construct the terraces on which the vines thrive to this day; facing south, they are protected from harsh winds. This section of the Wachau from Spitz down to Dürnstein (about 10 km., 6 miles) is the most beautiful and is devoted entirely to wine. Here Austria's noblest white wines grow: look out for Veltliners, Rheinrieslings and above all in Spitz for Neuburgers: they will all be aromatic but dry and light.

Visit the Hirtzberger Winery (02713–209). Try the "Steinfeder" (a new term for Wachau wines guaranteeing no added sugar and a maximum 10.7% alcohol content) *Grüner Veltliner Donaugarten 1984* and the superb *Riesling Spatlese Ried Hochrain 1983.* (When buying wine in the Wachau look for the insignia "Vinea Wachau Nobilis Districtus" on the label. Reputable growers in the area carry out their own strict quality control and this sign means the wine has passed more stringent tests than those set by the State. For instance, a "Federspiel" wine is equal to the Kabinett and must not exceed 11.9% alcohol.)

Time your journey so as to reach the tiny village of Weissenkirchen/Joching shortly before lunch. Don't miss the Franz Prager winery in Weissenkirchen (02 7 15–22 48) and compare two of his Veltliners from two different vineyards: *Hinter der Burg* and *Kaiserberg* in order to see how two wines of the same grape, grown within a few hundred yards of each other, can nevertheless be quite individual. Retain in your mind the taste of his Muscat Ottonel, dry and vigorous, to compare with one of its sweeter cousins in Burgenland. This vineyard is undoubtedly one of the finest in Austria. Having looked at the romantic village with its weathered Gothic church poised on a rock, you will only have to go one kilometer back to Joching where you can find lunch; and where better than at a wine "chateau," that of the Josef Jamek Winery (02 7 15–22 35, closed Sun. and Mon.)? Frau Jamek will cook a superbly light meal, using local ingredients and recipes. If you are lucky Herr Jamek will be on hand to guide you through his palette of wines: a young Veltliner might give way to a noble Rheinriesling which in turn could lead to his remarkable Pinot Blanc Spätlese, *Ried Hochrain:* fruity, yet absolutely dry. As you sip your coffee, round off your meal with his *Apricot Schnapps* before moving on.

It is only a few kilometers to Dürnstein where Richard the Lionheart was imprisoned. But this time, the aim is to seek out the Kellerschlössl, a Baroque palace designed by the great architect Jakob Prandtauer and home of the Dürnstein wine co-operative. While large co-operatives often exist to produce bulk wines, the one at Dürnstein has aimed at producing wines of the highest quality using the modern methods that only a co-operative can afford (02 7 11–22 17). The co-operative has a cellar capacity of 11 million liters at its disposal and you can taste the wines in the Vinothek wineshop in the little town (Tues. and Thurs. from 2.30 P.M. to 5). Compare a dry Neuburger *Ried Burgberg* with its fuller—some would say more characteristic—Neuburger *Ried Gut am Steg.* Don't miss their rich

Veltliner *Ried Lichtgartl* and a Rheinriesling Spätlese from the *Ried Kellerberg:* rich but never cloying.

A few kilometers on to Krems and the narrow valley has broadened and become gentler. Krems, one of the best preserved Baroque towns in Europe is also the home of the Lenz Moser family who did so much for the development of Austrian Wine after both World Wars. In town you can visit the Vinothek of the enormous wine co-operative, but perhaps you should seek out the Fritz Salomon Winery Undhof. Krems is right next door to a town called Stein and these used to be joined by a tiny community called *Und* (and). Hence the name Krems UND Stein. Und has long since been swallowed up, but the Undhof remains as proof. This vineyard is equal to that of Herr Prager in Weissenkirchen (02 7 32–32 26). Unforgettable is his Veltliner *Ried Wieden,* often considered Austria's finest. Try too his Rhein Riesling Spätlese *Ried Kremser Kögl.* Unusually for Austria, Herr Salomon has also experimented with the Pinot Gris grape; lovers of spicy wines will not want to miss his *Ried Wachtberg* Traminers.

The Wachau Tourist Office in Krems also arranges wine tours of the area, and at the beginning of June each year the Krems Wine Fair provides a unique opportunity to encounter many rare wines from the region. Worth noting, too, is the 1656 monastery of Und, now the first Austrian Wine Market. Restored last year, this has become the center of the Austrian Wine Market. For an entrance fee of AS120, you can taste wines from all over the country, take part in cultural events, and dine in a pleasant restaurant (tel. 02732–73074).

It might be wise to stay the night in Krems, across the river in Mautern at the Hotel Bacher. The restaurant is one of Austria's finest and the rooms are delightful. Liesl Wagner, here, was voted "cook of the year" in 1983 and she will cook you a delicate dinner worthy of the honor while her husband helps you choose from his fine Krems wines.

Next morning, take Route 218 out of Krems up to Langenlois. Beethoven liked to come and drink the white wine here and a visit to the Bründlmayer winery (02 7 34–21 72) quickly explains why. Here the wines are richer and fruitier, although not at all sweet; the soil and the flatter valley are the reason. Besides Veltliners and Rheinrieslings, the Bründlmayers have successfully experimented with red wines. Try their Blauburgunder (Pinot Noir) *Ried Dechant* as well as a Rheinriesling *Ried Zöbinger Heiligenstein.*

Leaving Langenlois, turn north up Route 34, following the River Kamp valley. At the end of this beautiful ride it is certainly worth visiting Rosenburg Castle, shortly before the town of Horn (35 km., 22 miles). In Horn take Route 45 to Pulkau and then Route 35 up to Retz, a distance of 29 km. (18 miles). Retz is the principal town of the *Weinviertel* or wine-district. This ancient town, still surrounded by its medieval walls, with superb patrician houses on the main square, is best visited at harvest-time. About then the barrels are emptied of old wine to prepare for the new and the fountain in the main square runs with wine! Beneath the town are 28 km. (17 miles) of cellar; you can visit these and refresh yourself at the end at an underground wine-bar. Retz is famous for good, rather heavier Veltliners but above all for its red wines: in Act II of the opera *Der Rosenkavalier* the wounded Baron Ochs is offered *Ein Retzer Wein* to make him feel better. He is delighted, and the ensuing waltz is proof of the wine's efficacy.

If there is time, visit the Weinbauschule (Viticultural College, 02 9 42–22 02) and compare a Blauer Portugieser *Ried Züngel Altenburg* with a Blauburger, also from the *Ried Züngel:* both are finely balanced and dry, the latter perhaps the fruitier and more velvety.

Leave Retz on a small road and drive through open, undulating country southeast to Haugsdorf. Notice in many of the villages the rows of cellars built into the sloping ground at the roadside. These cellar-streets, which are a feature of the area, called Kellergassen, are beautiful to look at and provide perfect storage conditions for the wines. In Haugsdorf you won't regret testing the red wines of the Josef Lust Winery (02 9 44–2 87). Compare his *Roter Fasan* Blauer Portugieser with his Pinot Noir. The former grape is so often used to make mass-market wines that a taste of Herr Lust's Blauer Portugiesers comes as a revelation.

Inns to stay in in this area are simple, but all will provide clean, comfortable accommodation and good local food at amazingly low prices. From Haugsdorf travel east along Route 45 to Laa an der Thaya, and join Route 46; this road brings you to the amazing castle of Staatz, perched high on its volcanic rock. A walk up to the ruins will prepare you for the next round of tastings! From Staatz, Route 219 brings you to Poysdorf, about 50 km. (31 miles) altogether from Haugsdorf.

In Poysdorf, centre of the Falkenstein wine district, call at the Gunter Haimer Winery (02 5 52–25 59). In an area often given to mass production he has placed his cards on quality: beautiful Kabinett Veltliners lead one on to his exceptional *Ried Taubenschuss,* a dry Veltliner Spätlese. This wine is proof of what the Veltliner grape is capable of. Also in Poysdorf you can, if you give advance notice, enjoy a gourmet tasting at the Franz Rieder Winery in Kleinhadersdorf-Poysdorf, Untere Ortsstrasse 44 (02552–2241). AS250 per person for ten or more.

Traveling straight down towards Vienna you have the amazing sight of vines growing round endless oil-wells. Here are Austria's largest oil-fields: the two life-bloods exist, happily, side by side—a truly Austrian solution of life's problems.

The Wine Trail Continues

Now, leave Vienna to the west and travel on south to Gumpoldskirchen. This tiny village on the eastern slopes of the last Alpine rocks has lived for wine for two thousand years. It produces the richest, most magnificent white wines in Austria and their fame is widespread. At one stage, there was more Gumpoldskirchner on the world markets than the village could ever have produced—a situation reminiscent of the medieval glut of pieces of the True Cross; in self defense the growers introduced strict measures of control. Always look for the words *Original Gumpoldskirchner* on the bottle. The further word *Königswein* (Wine of Kings) means that the bottle in question is a particularly special wine. But do go easy on the intake— Gumpoldskirchner wines are heavier and go straight to the head.

Stroll down the main street on a warm evening and call in at any of the houses displaying a bunch of fir twigs at the door. Such a house is open for wine and cold food; the courtyard behind the house, usually protected by a huge old tree, will make you linger.

It is here that the Zierpfandler and the Rotgipfler grapes come into their own. Just outside Gumpoldskirchen is the Thallern Winery, belonging to the Heiligenkreuz monastery in the southern Vienna Woods. Try a Zierpfandler *Ried Wiege,* Auslese and Beerenauslese or a golden *Rotgipfler Trockenbeerenauslese.* The winery has a tiny Gothic chapel housing a *Christ on the Vine* by Heiligenkreuz sculptor Giuliani.

By now you will probably need to spend the night in Baden to the south before going on to Bad Vöslau. Here look for the Robert Schlumberger Winery (02 2 52–72 90). This Alsatian family came from the Champagne to Austria in 1845 and were instrumental in starting the production of sparkling wines in Austria. Although no longer made by him, the *Ultra Brut* (sparkling wine) that bears his name is undoubtedly Austria's finest brand of Sekt.

The Schlumbergers are famous for their red wines; indeed one of these was served to Queen Victoria at the Great Exhibition of 1862. She liked it so much that the wine was put on her Kensington Palace wine-list. Remarkable is the Schlumberger *Privatkeller* Cabernet-Merlot; here Herr Schlumberger has used the two great Bordeaux grapes, almost unique in Austria.

From Vöslau take Route 305 east across to Ebreichsdorf where you join Route 16 from Vienna down to Eisenstadt. This jewel of a town, made famous by the Esterhazys and Josef Haydn, is the capital of the Burgenland. You could do worse than stay at the new Hotel Burgenland since from here you can make trips out to Lake Neusiedl. Around this steppe lake, unique in Europe, you can travel north towards Neusiedl and around into the Seewinkel, a huge nature reserve and bird sanctuary. The wine here is good and plentiful. Call in at any house with the *Flaschenwein* sign and ask to taste.

All the Burgenland wines bear the mark of an area that was part of Hungary until after World War I. The wines, as is inevitable in a warm climate, have in the past tended to be heavy and sweet, but enterprising young growers are now producing dry wines of real depth. The Anton Kollwentz Winery, 7051 Grosshöflein (02 6 82/51 58) produces some magnificent *barrique*-matured reds. Don't miss Donnerskirchen, 14 km. (8½ miles) northeast of Eisenstadt on Route 304. A good lunch at the Restaurant Engel will prepare you for a tasting at the St. Martinus co-operative in the village. This co-operative has aimed at a lighter style, reflected in their dry Welschrieslings. It also holds informative wine seminars. Try also Spätlese and Trockenbeerenauslese from the Welschriesling and the Muscat-Ottonel grapes and think back to Herr Prager's Muscat Ottonel many tastings ago in Weissenkirchen. Here too you might finally have the chance to try an Eiswein.

Another outing will take you to the free town of Rust. Unspoilt, this town offers shelter to several families of storks who arrive from Egypt every spring and spend the summer there. A cold lunch in the Rathauskeller can be combined with an on-the-spot tasting of countless local wines.

After a good night's sleep, Route 331 will take you south from Eisenstadt for about 30 km. (18½ miles) to Weppersdorf and there turn east on Route 62 to go about 20 km. (12½ miles) to Deutschkreuz. Make straight for the Hans Igler Winery (02 6 13–365), for Herr Igler has invested his time, his love and his money in creating red wines of international distinction. His Blaufränkisch Kabinett from various barrels emerge the winners at every tasting, year after year.

Returning to Route 61, go for another 26 km. (16 miles) south until you turn off on Route 55 west to Lockenhaus. Here, after a pause to enjoy the scenery, go south on Route 56 and follow the Hungarian border through Rechnitz about 40 km. (25 miles) down to Eisenberg. At this point the lovely wooded steppes open out eastwards to reveal a small, steep area of sloping vineyards facing southeast. These look down past the border watchtowers onto the Hungarian plains. At the foot of the Eisenberg is the village of Deutsch Schützen. Call ahead to the Körper Winery (03365–2203) just outside the village. Herr Körper has an amazing selection of white wines which he will happily open for you to taste. It is his reds, however, from the Eisenberg that are unforgettable. Compare his Blaufränkisch with his Zweigelt, the former being the rounder without in any way being heavy or cloying. His Merlot grape experiments have had remarkable results and 1989 should see his first Cabernet vintage.

Before leaving the Burgenland, spend a night at the Hotel Raffel in Jennersdorf, 30 km. (18½ miles) southwest on Route 57. A comfortable room will await you after a Pannonian dinner of gargantuan proportions, served stylishly in a dining-room of elegance. Herr Kampel, the owner, will enjoy advising you in making a choice from his extensive cellar.

Around 20 km. (12½ miles) south of Jennersdorf you are already well into Styria by the time you get to Klöch, where a visit to the Ducal Stürgkh Winery (03 4 75–223) is a must. Here, on a tiny area, grow Gewürztraminers equal to those of Alsace. Start with the Kabinetts and move on to the *Kellerbraut* Spätlese, in hand-numbered bottles. You will find it justifies its fame as one of the finest in Europe.

Follow the little road south till you come to Route 69, then travel along the River Mur and the Yugoslav border for 30 km. (18½ miles), crossing the main north–south road at Strass. When you reach Ehrenhausen, turn south onto the South Styrian Wine Road. Soon you are on the border with Yugoslavia, literally *on,* half the road is in Yugoslavia and half in Austria! On either side endless vineyards fall away steeply. These are some of the steepest vineyards in the world and have to be worked by hand. Look out for a *Klapotetz,* a large wind-operated moving scarecrow designed to keep the birds off the grapes. To work, they say, these must be made of cherrywood: you may be lucky and hear one in action.

Output here is not great, but the wines have finesse and richness. Drive slowly, for the road is narrow and twisty, but also to enjoy the unique scenery as beautiful as any wine country in the world. Stop at one of the many *Buschenschanks* and order a Brettljause (a board with cold meats, bread and pickles); try a Welschriesling with it, or a Morillon or a Traminer. Then sit and forget the world outside, which you can do here, for people even forget there is a border; just drink in the view, the wine and the peace. One warning: don't go at the weekend, for most of the citizens of Graz have the same idea.

Rejoin Route 69 at Leutschach, turn right at Arnfels and follow the valley up to Route 74 (about 10 km., 6 miles). Here a small road leads up to the village of Kitzeck, the highest wine-village in Europe, whose sloping vineyards will make you dizzy if you look down. There is a tiny wine-museum, a local labour of love, that is well worth a visit.

From Kitzeck, travel 30 km. (18½ miles) westwards to Deutschlandsberg and join Route 76 leading up to Stainz. Between these towns on the slopes to our left, grows a grape found nowhere else in the world: the Blauer Wildbacher. From this is made a wine called *Schilcher.* This rosé wine, always drunk chilled, is anything from onion-skin colored round Stainz, to a fuller red-pink nearer Deutschlandsberg; the wine is tangy, heady and sometimes almost sour. For many it is an acquired, or not ac-

quired taste, but it is certainly one not to miss. A Schilcher Wine Road
has been created and maps are available from the village tourist office
(03462–2377). Various *Gasthauses* and *Buschenschanks* have joined to
offer the finest wines and traditional local dishes. A particularly fine Schilcher is produced by E. & M. Müller at vineyards belonging to the Liechtenstein family. Their winery is at Gross St. Florian (03 4 64–234) and
their *Ried Burgegg* Schilcher has the true onion-skin colour. Indeed, for
a cross section of what Styria has to offer, this winery is ideal for a visit.

End of the Trail

And so you have traveled through most of Austria's wine country and
finally return to Vienna. What other capital city has vineyards within its
bounds? The *Heuriger* (this year's wine) Taverns of Grinzing, Sievering
and Nussdorf are lodestones for wine lovers. It is a memorable experience
to sit at the edge of a vineyard on the Kahlenberg with a tankard of young
white wine, and listen to the *Schrammel* quartet playing sentimental Viennese songs. How far-sighted of the Emperor Joseph to decree in 1784 that
winegrowers could sell their wines together with cold food direct to cus-
tomers whenever they liked. At the same time, the Viennese discovered
that it was cheaper to go out to the wine than to bring it inside the city
walls where taxes were levied. Mutual interest has thus made an institution
of these *Heurigen.*

There are so many of these taverns, that it would be frivolous to single
any out: everyone in Vienna has his favorite which is also of course the
best. Beethoven, however, knew a good thing when he lived at a house
on the Pfarrplatz in Heiligenstadt for some time. Now belonging to the
Mayer family, it houses a Heuriger which really serves its own wines (37
12 87, open daily from 4 P.M.) and has long been a favourite of many famous Viennese. If you go there in the fall, try a glass of *Sturm,* a cloudy
drink halfway between grape-juice and wine, with a delicious yeasty fizz.
Ing. Mayer also owns vineyards within Vienna that produce some wines
of exceptional quality: try his *Alsegger* Rheinriesling, steely and dry and
compare this with another Rheinriesling, *Schwarze Katz* from the Nuss-
berg. This second is mellower and they make an interesting contrast, coming as they do from different districts of Vienna.

On your last evening, call a taxi and ask him to take you to Heuriger
Sirbu (37 13 19, closed Sun.) on the Kahlenbergerstrasse at the *Eiserner
Hand.* Here on a slope high above the Danube, with a tankard of exceptionally good *Heuriger* and a plateful of cold food in front of you, you
can sit beneath a trellis of vines and glimpse the stars above. Away to your
left are the upper reaches of the Kahlenberg, once occupied by the Turks,
and below you Vienna and the Danube, lights sparkling as the dusk turns
to night. Way across the other side, just visible, are the lights of Bisamberg,
another wine village we haven't even begun to talk about . . .

A Wine Vocabulary

In order to help you find your way through the maze of bottles, *viertels*
and barrels of this long liquid adventure, here are a few of the simpler
words that are used in the delicious world of Austrian wine.

Abgang	aftertaste
blumig	with a fine bouquet
dünn	watery, thin
feurig	heady
fruchtig	fruity
herb	dry
Körper	body
körperreich	full-bodied
leicht	light
moussierend	sparkling
rassig	aromatic, fragrant
resch	crisp, lively, dry
sauer	sour, sharp, rough
schwer	full-bodied, heady
spritzig	slightly sparkling because young
Ein Spritzer	wine mixed with mineral water
süffig	pleasant to drink
süss	sweet
trocken	dry
Ein Viertel	¼ of a liter, served open
Weinstein	Residual acid crystals in dry white wine. A sure sign of high quality

MUSIC IN AUSTRIA

The Year-Round Festival

by
KENNETH LOVELAND

One of Britain's senior music critics and a well-known travel writer, Kenneth Loveland has spent more than half-a-century in journalism, being at one time national President of the Guild of British Newspaper Editors. He now devotes himself to writing and broadcasting entirely about music. His love affair with Austria goes back many years—including nearly 30 consecutive Salzburg Festivals.

For the musical tourist who is excited at the prospect of treading in the footprints of the mighty, seeing where masterpieces were committed to paper, or standing where a long-loved work was either praised or damned at its first appearance, Austria is tops. The land is saturated with musical history.

The fact that a composer was born in a certain house does not of itself make that house interesting, though the contents, if it has become a museum, will attract. Indeed, most composers moved from their birthplace before reaching their creative years. Far more stimulating to see where they worked, to see the surroundings in which a symphony came to life, to see where the music itself was born. Austria has more of this to the square kilometer than anywhere else in the world. And Vienna is the heart of it all.

MUSIC IN AUSTRIA **101**

There is a tram starting from the center of Vienna which runs past the house where Mozart wrote his last three symphonies. Look left, and you will see the end of the street in which Beethoven died, and from which his funeral cortege set out. A young man named Schubert, so tragically soon to go on the same journey, was among the torch-bearers. A little further on, and you will pass the house where he was born. A little further, a house where Beethoven worked, and the journey ends on the edge of the Vienna woods, hymned by Johann Strauss the younger.

Leave the tram, and it is a short walk to the house from which Beethoven set out on that hike which produced the *Pastoral Symphony.* Progress, that relentless mauler of illusions, has dipped its itchy fingers into some of the countryside. But you can still follow that same walk, still find the brook which inspired the slow movement, and on a spring morning, the air will be filled with bird song just as Beethoven found it. And on a fine Sunday afternoon, scores of faithful Viennese will be seen following the trail. It matters. It is inheritance.

The end of that tram ride is haunted by Beethoven. Have a glass of wine in the garden of a tavern where he lodged, then walk the short distance to the house where he wrote that heart-broken testament when he discovered that his deafness was incurable.

Only a hard-boiled cynic can fail to be moved. And back in Vienna itself, only the flint-hearted can stand in the Währingerstrasse and look at the windows behind which Mozart wrote those last three symphonies in the incredible short time of six weeks in the summer of 1788 and not be touched. For this was the time when the Mozart fortunes had slumped to their lowest, the begging letters to their most pathetic. Next year, Mozart was to write to a friend "If you, my best of friends, forsake me, I am unhappily and innocently lost with my poor sick wife and my child." But then Vienna is neither for the hard-boiled nor the flint-hearted. It is for the musical romantic, happy to be where names and events come to life. And so is all of Austria, over which the Vienna tradition cast its influence, and still does.

Strangers in Town

Mozart, Schubert, Beethoven, Haydn, Richard Strauss, Mahler, Bruckner, Lehár, Johann Strauss II, Brahms—what a list they make. Yet hardly any of those who built the Vienna tradition were Viennese themselves, some not even Austrian.

Mozart came there on a visit from Salzburg with his employer, the Archbishop Hieronymus von Colloredo. The Archbishop sacked him, and got his unenviable place in history as the man who fired the most versatile composer who ever lived (he must have been, mustn't he? Those operas, symphonies, piano concertos, all that chamber music, crammed into a life that ended when he was only 35). And Mozart stayed in Vienna.

Beethoven came from the Rhineland, Haydn from Lower Austria, Brahms from Germany, Mahler from Bohemia, Bruckner from Upper Austria, Lehár from Hungary, Richard Strauss from Bavaria. Only Schubert and Johann Strauss II were Viennese-born.

So what were they doing there?

Vienna was the capital of the Habsburg empire, and it was an empire in which music ran strong. The aristocracy not only patronized it, giving employment and commissions to composers. Many of them were skilful musicians themselves. We owe much to those overlords. Let us be grateful for Beethoven's encouragement from the Archduke Rudolph, to Prince Lobkowitz for his patient support of Beethoven, to Prince Lichnowsky (in whose palace Beethoven astutely found lodgings when he arrived in Vienna), to Count Waldstein, to Count Rasoumovsky of the quartets, and those other noblemen who stand behind so much that has come down to us.

Stroll round Vienna, and it is fascinating to think of Beethoven walking there, hands thrust behind him, chin jutting out.

The stories of his deafness range from the comic to the sad. When conducting, he would crouch low in a quiet passage, then suddenly leap in the air for the *crescendo* he could not hear. At the end of the first performance of the *Ninth Symphony,* the ovation was tremendous. Then the mezzo soloist, Karolina Unger, realizing that he knew nothing of it, turned Beethoven round gently, and led him to the front of the platform so that he could see the audience on their feet, cheering and waving hats.

Never embarrass a Viennese policeman by asking where Beethoven lived. The list is too long. He moved all the time. But many of the places associated with him are easily tracked down. The Pasqualati House up on the Molkerbastei, where he wrote much of *Fidelio,* the fourth, fifth and sixth symphonies, has survived the march of time, and so have several others. The Kärntnertortheatre, where the *Ninth Symphony* was first heard, stood on the site now occupied by Sacher's of the delicious cakes, but the palace of Prince Lobkowitz, where the *Eroica Symphony* was first rehearsed, is much as it was in Beethoven's time.

Schubert haunts yield themselves less easily, but are there for the seeking. Many of his songs were written for those parties of artistic friends gathered around him, some for the baritone Johann Michael Vogl, sung perhaps just once or twice, then placed on one side. Yet they included many of the finest ever written. Some have never been recovered. How many gems as precious as *An die Musik, Erlkönig,* or *An Silvia* were among the manuscripts we are told were used to light a fire after his death? Some which had been discarded surfaced years later to become eternally popular. No other great composer can owe his fame today to so much music that came to light posthumously.

He never heard his *Symphony No. 9,* the great C major, today an essential in the repertory of any important orchestra. In rehearsal, the musicians of Vienna found it too difficult and it was withdrawn. Ten years after his death, Schubert's brother Ferdinand sent it to Schumann, who passed it on for Mendelssohn to give it in Leipzig in 1839. For years conductors were deterred by its length. When it was introduced to London, August Manns played for safety by spreading it over two evenings. And Vienna? They played it there at last in 1839, but only the first two movements were given, and they were separated by a Donizetti aria. The imagination wilts.

But strange things happened at concerts in Vienna in the first half of the 19th century. Nothing stranger than that which occurred at the first performance of Beethoven's *Violin Concerto* at the Theater an der Wien on December 23, 1806. Beethoven had been late finishing it, and Franz Clement played it from manuscript. It seems not to have upset him. For good measure, he threw in between the first two movements a sonata of his own played on one string with the violin held upside down.

They had prodigious appetites, too. What about the concert that was given in the same theater on December 22, 1808? It contained what today would be called the world premieres of Beethoven's *Symphony No. 5,* his *Pastoral Symphony,* and his *Piano Concerto No. 4.* Has any single concert ever bequeathed so much music destined to be universally loved?

For the discovery of Schubert's *Unfinished Symphony* we move to Graz in Styria. In 1865, the Viennese conductor Johann Herbeck went there to inquire if Anselm Hüttenbrunner, once a friend of Schubert's, had any of Schubert's manuscripts. The tired old man rummaged in a chest, and produced a mass of papers. Herbeck saw among them a symphony in B minor. "Take it" said Anselm. "There's no hurry to return it." And that is how what is one of the best-known of all symphonies came to light 37 years after its composer's death.

Of all the composers who died young, Schubert is most to be mourned. He was only 31, and his last works show a face turned resolutely forward. As it was, the mantle of succession to Beethoven fell on Brahms. A realist in all things, he accepted the fact, but was cautious about admitting it. "I shall never compose a symphony" he wrote to a friend. "You have no conception of how the likes of us feel when we hear the tramp of a giant like Beethoven behind us." But his first symphony proclaimed that the tradition would go on.

Musical Establishments

I never sit in Vienna's Musikverein without stealing a glance at the balcony and visualizing the scene that day, March 7, 1897, when the Vienna Philharmonic played Brahms's *Symphony No. 4.* Death was already waiting for him, and the Brahms who limped to the front of the artist's box was shrunken and haggard, the hair hanging lank. He bowed slowly to the cheering audience, and walked slowly away. Within a month he was dead, but he had carried away the adoration of an audience who knew they would never see him again.

But the Viennese have not always been kind. They were slow to recognize the genius of Bruckner, and have often given a rough time to composers or musicians on whom they at first lavished acclamation. Mahler, who arrived as conductor of the Court Opera (now the Vienna State) in 1897, brought about numerous reforms, built a brilliant ensemble, and gave Vienna a golden decade which is still discussed. But he made enemies, and worn out by intrigues, eventually left for America.

Neither have the Viennese always been shrewd judges of imported music. Musical history is littered with examples of works which flopped with a resounding thud then bounced back to popularity to the embarrassment of the original critics. The first performance of the Tchaikovsky *Violin Concerto* took place in Vienna at a Philharmonic concert on December 4, 1881, with Adolf Brodsky as soloist. There was much hissing, and Eduard Hanslick, the leading Viennese critic of the time, stalked from the hall to describe the concerto as "stinking in the ear." Wrote Hanslick "We see wild and vulgar faces, we hear curses, we smell bad brandy." But there are not many surer crowd-pullers today.

We have begun to mention the famous Viennese musical institutions, and it is time to consider them in more detail.

The Vienna State Opera is more than just a theater. It is a visual symbol of Vienna's pride in its own status and achievements. They say that when it burned after the bombing of March 13, 1945, hundreds of people who had never ventured inside wept in the streets. To them, it *was* Vienna.

The theater had a chequered early career. It owed its existence to the foresight of the Emperor Franz Josef and his ministers who demolished the walls surrounding the inner city to make way for a wide boulevard fringed by splendid buildings. One of these was to be a new opera house. A competition for the design was won by Eduard van der Nüll and August Siccard von Siccardsburg. But things were going badly for Austria at this time, and both the expense of the new opera house and its design were useful targets for attack. Eduard van der Nüll hung himself, and Siccardsburg died of a stroke soon after.

But the theater was soon famous. First Richter, then Mahler brought standards to the height of perfection. And despite the ruin of World War I, the Vienna State Opera (as the former Vienna Court Opera now became), enjoyed another golden era in the 1920s with singers like Slezak, Mayr, Lehmann, Schumann and Tauber. The political events of the 1930s, then World War II, took their toll, and in 1944, with the Allies fighting in Normandy, it was decided that the theater should not re-open for the next season. The following year, it lay in ruins. The last opera performed there, prophetically, had been *Götterdämerung.* Yet when it was re-built, a new generation of great singers ushered in another golden era. Mahler had once declared that tradition was slovenliness, but on a night when everything is going well at the Vienna State, one is conscious of the best that tradition implies, something handed down.

The Volksoper is to operetta what the Staatsoper is to opera. And this is the point at which to emphasise that operetta is not just a junior branch of opera. Thank heavens, this truth, which the Austrians have always understood, is now generally accepted in civilized musical circles throughout the world. As works of art, as examples of musical-theater craftsmanship, operettas like *The Merry Widow, Die Fledermaus* and *The Gipsy Baron* stand infinitely higher than some of the operas through which, as a critic, I am often condemned to sit. And it cannot be a coincidence that the finest singers of Viennese operetta have always been the greatest Mozart singers, the greatest Schubert *lieder* singers. The genuine operetta sound, stylish and cultured, descends in the same line. One thinks of Schumann and Tauber in the past, Schwarzkopf in our own time.

But somehow, I feel always that where the ghosts of the Vienna tradition walk most surely is the Theater an der Wien. Schikaneder, that remarkable showman who was Papageno in the first production of *The Magic Flute* in 1791, built it soon after and it was under his management when *Fidelio* was first performed there. Beethoven lived in it for a while, and as we have seen, much of his music was first heard there.

Its succeeding history is colorful. Barbaia, the former waiter who once managed Naples's San Carlo Theatre where a share of the profits of the royal gaming tables was written into his contract, was one manager. Another was Count Palffy, who hit on a shrewd money-making scheme. He decided to raffle the theater, with the proviso that if the winner did not want it, he could have 300,000 gulden instead. A countryman won, and decided to take the cash, which meant that the Count had made a handsome financial profit and still kept the theatre. But the winner had, if not an outright last laugh, at least a farewell chuckle. He insisted on being paid in 20 gulden pieces. The last we hear of him is setting off for home with the coins loaded on a wagon, and accompanied by an escort of police for safety.

Operetta gave the Theater an der Wien a splendid epoch much later in the 19th century. Offenbach brought his French operettas to Vienna in 1863, triumphed, and the Viennese just had to find an answer. They found it in the enchanting works of Zeller, Millöcker, Suppé, and in particular Johann Strauss II, already famous throughout the world as the Waltz King. Many of the most famous Viennese operettas were first given at the Theater an der Wien, among them *Die Fledermaus* (1874), *The Gipsy Baron* (1885) and *Waldmeister* (1895) all by Johann. As the century died, it seemed that operetta in Vienna would die with it, as first one then another of its composers passed away, Suppé in 1895, Zeller in 1898, Johann Strauss in 1899. Millöcker just failed to make the new century, dying on December 31, 1899.

Then in 1905, Lehár's *The Merry Widow* opened at the Theater an der Wien. Lehár was not the first choice, and picked up the libretto only after others had turned it down. Neither did it succeed at first. But its eventual popularity led to an operetta revival, and paved the way for a new generation of composers, among whom Kalman, with *The Gipsy Princess* (1915) and *Countess Maritza* (1924) and Oscar Strauss with *A Waltz Dream* (1907) were important. Today, Viennese operetta is enjoying success with a new audience, who are finding its eloquent tunes and insinuating rhythms a delightful experience.

The Theater an der Wien has been beautifully restored to look as it did in Beethoven's time. It plays a major role in the annual Vienna Festival. One of the most memorable nights of my life was spent listening to *Fidelio* on the stage where it was first played, on the very night of the 200th anniversary of the composer's birth.

The Vienna Philharmonic, that other radiant jewel in the Austrian musical crown, has a double function, spending part of its time playing for the Vienna State Opera, and giving its regular symphony concerts in the Musikverein on Sunday mornings. Its identifying characteristic (every great orchestra has one) is the beauty of its string tone. It was formed by Nicolai (of *The Merry Wives of Windsor*) in 1842.

Music in the Blood

In Austria, music is for delight as well as inspiration. The statue of Johann Strauss II in the Stadtpark tells all. To see him, violin tucked under the chin, is to imagine those infectious waltzes, *Wine, Women and Song, Voices of Spring,* and best of them all, the *Emperor.* But quite possibly you will not need to imagine them. Somewhere in the distance, an orchestra will be playing them, somewhere heads will be swaying, feet will be tapping. Johann wrote a waltz called *Wiener Blut,* but he might just as well have called it Austrian Blood, for music is in the blood of all the people, whether it echoes from *Don Giovanni* at the State Opera or the Viennese waltzes it gave to the world.

Johann was a fine musician (though he thought his brother Josef was a better one) and worked some adventurous things into his programs. On the night he lay dying, his orchestra was giving an openair concert, and someone tip-toed up to the stand to whisper to the leader. The orchestra stopped, then started to play, very quietly, *The Blue Danube.* And Vienna knew the waltz king had died.

The Vienna Festival takes place in May and June. They call it the festival of 1,000 performances. Into this shop window, Vienna puts the best that Austria can offer as well as playing host to orchestras, opera companies, ballets and famous musicians from all over the world.

Then there is that other Viennese specialty. On a fine evening, seek out the taverns of Grinzing or Heiligenstadt. As the shadows deepen and the lights appear under the trees, a quartet will start to play *Schrammelmusik,* those sentimental, nostalgic songs peculiar to Vienna. Sip the new wine, enjoy the cold meats served with it, and do what the Viennese do. Relax and just let it happen.

But this is starting to look as though music in Austria is mostly a Viennese experience. It is not, but the point is that all the thriving musical life you will find in the provinces somehow flows from the Viennese source. Neither should it be assumed that music in Austria lives entirely in the past. After all, Vienna is where Schönberg, Berg and Webern started the atonal revolution from which few seriously creative composers have been able to escape uninfluenced since.

The Salzburg Festival represents everything that is splendid in its preservation of the operas of Mozart in the city of his birth, and holds a mirror every year to Austria's orchestral heritage. But even Salzburg finds room for experiment. This is where Henze's *The Bassarids* first appeared in 1966, and where Friedrich Cerha's *Baal* had its world premiere in 1981. Cerha's great contribution, of course, has been to complete Berg's unfinished *Lulu.* In 1971, the Vienna Festival brought out Gottfried von Einem's *The Visit of the Old Lady,* one of the more successful new operas of recent years.

But the crowds who throng Salzburg at festival time are mostly there to honor tradition. Mozart's music must be one of the biggest revenue earners the Austrians have. There are nights when one watches the crowds pouring over the bridge across the Salzach on their way, perhaps, to *Cosi Fan Tutte* or *The Marriage of Figaro;* nights when one sees the coaches lined up outside the best hotels to take visitors to the festival theaters, or notes tickets changing hands at black market prices, sees the shops stocked with Mozart souvenirs, and then the cruel irony strikes home. The reason for it, the reason this lovely city is packed with visitors, went to a pauper's grave.

Salzburg and Vienna, they lead the world's festivals. But Austria teems with festivals. Many with contrasted themes. Graz, in October, is about the future. The names I see on the program in front of me are Kagel, Ligeti, Cerha.

The Austrians are skilled at calling up nature to help with the staging. The Bregenz Festival, tucked into that corner of the Vorarlberg where the borders of Austria, Germany and Switzerland tumble over each other, uses a floating stage on Lake Constance, whose shores house the openair audience. The sky darkens, the moon rises, the lights of Lindau on the German shore twinkle, a steamer glides in the distance, and it is all romance—aquatic opera under the stars. Linz, in the early autumn, naturally exploits its proud association with Bruckner, who was at one time organist in the city's cathedral.

Somehow, in Austria, everything seems to come back to music. Who can visit the Burgenland without recalling Haydn and his almost 30 years' service for Prince Nicholas Esterhazy, surely one of the happiest patron-composer relationships in all music? The mountains of the Tirol somehow suggest the proud peaks of a Bruckner symphony, a leisured moment in a Viennese coffee house the nonchalant near-sentimentality of a Schubert impromptu, a picnic by a Carinthian lake the prospect of Brahms sketching a symphony during one of those working holidays he so enjoyed there, a stroll through the park at Bad Ischl, beloved of Lehar, prompts in the mind a tune that really belongs to Hanna Glawari.

It was in a tavern in the Burgenland that I congratulated the waitress, cheerful, fresh in her local costume, on the quality of a meal. She thought. "Austrian cooking" she said "is a symphony in a frying pan." Now, I wonder where she read that. But the remark told a story. In Austria, search for a metaphor and you are bound to come up with something musical.

INDEX

Index

Practical Information for Austria

Practical Information for Vienna

Geographical Index for Vienna and The Wine Road

Fodor's Travel Guides

U.S. Guides

Alaska
Arizona
Atlantic City & the
  New Jersey Shore
Boston
California
Cape Cod
Carolinas & the
  Georgia Coast
The Chesapeake Region
Chicago
Colorado
Disney World & the
  Orlando Area

Florida
Hawaii
Las Vegas
Los Angeles, Orange
  County, Palm Springs
Maui
Miami,
  Fort Lauderdale,
  Palm Beach
Michigan, Wisconsin,
  Minnesota
New England
New Mexico
New Orleans

New Orleans (Pocket
  Guide)
New York City
New York City (Pocket
  Guide)
New York State
Pacific North Coast
Philadelphia
The Rockies
San Diego
San Francisco
San Francisco (Pocket
  Guide)
The South

Texas
USA
Virgin Islands
Virginia
Waikiki
Washington, DC

Foreign Guides

Acapulco
Amsterdam
Australia, New Zealand,
  The South Pacific
Austria
Bahamas
Bahamas (Pocket
  Guide)
Baja & the Pacific
  Coast Resorts
Barbados
Beijing, Guangzhou &
  Shanghai
Belgium &
  Luxembourg
Bermuda
Brazil
Britain (Great Travel
  Values)
Budget Europe
Canada
Canada (Great Travel
  Values)
Canada's Atlantic
  Provinces
Cancun, Cozumel,
  Yucatan Peninsula

Caribbean
Caribbean (Great
  Travel Values)
Central America
Eastern Europe
Egypt
Europe
Europe's Great
  Cities
France
France (Great Travel
  Values)
Germany
Germany (Great Travel
  Values)
Great Britain
Greece
The Himalayan
  Countries
Holland
Hong Kong
Hungary
India,
  including Nepal
Ireland
Israel
Italy

Italy (Great Travel
  Values)
Jamaica
Japan
Japan (Great Travel
  Values)
Kenya, Tanzania,
  the Seychelles
Korea
Lisbon
Loire Valley
London
London (Great
  Travel Values)
London (Pocket Guide)
Madrid & Barcelona
Mexico
Mexico City
Montreal &
  Quebec City
Munich
New Zealand
North Africa
Paris
Paris (Pocket Guide)
People's Republic of
  China

Portugal
Rio de Janeiro
The Riviera (Fun on)
Rome
Saint Martin &
  Sint Maarten
Scandinavia
Scandinavian Cities
Scotland
Singapore
South America
South Pacific
Southeast Asia
Soviet Union
Spain
Spain (Great Travel
  Values)
Sweden
Switzerland
Sydney
Tokyo
Toronto
Turkey
Vienna
Yugoslavia

Special-Interest Guides

Health & Fitness
  Vacations
Royalty Watching

Selected Hotels of
  Europe

Selected Resorts and
  Hotels of the U.S.
Shopping in Europe

Skiing in North America
Sunday in New York